Inside the Presidency:

The Trials & Tribulations of a Zambian Spin Doctor

Dickson Jere

Former Spokesman for Zambian's Fourth President,

Rupiah Banda

Copyright © 2014 Dickson Jere
All rights reserved.

This publication may not be reproduced, in whole or in part, by any means including photocopying or using any information storage or retrieval system, without specific and prior written permission of the publisher.

This book is sold subject to the condition that it shall not, by way of trade or otherwise, be re-sold, hired out, or otherwise circulated without the publisher's prior consent in any form of binding or cover other than that in which it is published and without a similar condition including this condition being imposed on the subsequent purchaser.

Every effort has been made to trace copyright holders of material reproduced in this book. No infringements are intended and if any (through inadvertent action) happened, necessary corrections would be made in future editions.

First Edition: April 2012

Published by: Nsemia Inc. Publishers (www.nsemia.com); Oakville, Ontario, Canada

Edited by Charles Phebih-Agyekum
Cover Concept by Dickson Jere
Cover Design by Robert Chaponda
Cover Layout Design by Daniel Pitt
Layout Design by Kemunto Matunda
Author Picture by Rancen

Note for Librarians: a cataloguing record for this book is available from Library and Archives Canada.

ISBN: 978-1-926906-36-2

DEDICATION

To my children, Siyabonga, Khuzwayo and Mandhla

ACKNOWLEDGEMENTS

There are many people who encouraged me to write this book immediately after I left State House where I served as Chief Policy Analyst and eventually Special Assistant to the President for Press and Public Relations. I am grateful for the encouragement, which has led to its realization.

I am thankful to former President Mr. Rupiah Bwezani Banda for having taken time from his busy schedule to read through the manuscript and providing invaluable feedback. He reminded me of some of the projects he personally initiated which I did not include in my earlier drafts.

I am particularly indebted to veteran journalist Arthur Simuchoba who endured long hours of going through the draft chapters and provided a key critique of the manuscript. He also raised some issues that helped the narrative.

Thanks to my Ivorian friend Vincent Tobhi who went through some of the chapters and provided valuable feedback. The same goes to my peer review team of friends, Soche Zulu and Obert Simwanza, for the time they took in reviewing the chapters. I would also like to recognize the input from Sara Guenet Banda who made initial comments to the earlier chapters when I started writing this book.

Finally, thanks go to my publishers who believed in the book and managed to put it where it is today. I say thank you all.

PREFACE

When I decided to write my memoirs based on my experience working in State House, there was a great deal of skepticism among those who came to know of my intention. Some said I was too young to write memoirs while others thought three-years in State House was too short a period to write a book. But there were also those who thought I had a good story to tell.

I personally thought I had gained valuable knowledge, insights and experiences that I needed to share. I was at the centre of events that shaped our country's history including being witness to a peaceful transfer of power from an incumbent to the in-coming former opposition leader- a rare phenomenon in Africa.

I have tried in this book to explain and describe in as much detail as possible the trials and tribulations of a Zambian Presidential spokesman based on my experiences. Of course my experiences may differ from those of my predecessors and those who will come after me as they will work with different presidents with different leadership styles. But some of the challenges are likely to be the same.

I have not been able to provide much detail to some events because of the two oaths I took; of office and allegiance. They require that I maintain secrecy even after leaving office. I have therefore been unable to discuss a number of pertinent issues especially those pertaining to defence and security matters as well as internal meetings and decisions.

I have deliberately used official titles and offices instead of naming individuals unless where it was absolutely necessary because I wanted to discuss and describe events rather than persons.

I am sure my documented experience and account in this book may not be the same as those of other aides who served during my time at State House. They are of course free to differ by writing their version of events.

For now, I leave it to you the readers to enjoy the pages that follow. It is my wish that this book helps broaden knowledge on how Zambian presidents work as well as be a window on Zambian and African politics at the time.

Dickson Jere

TABLE OF CONTENTS

DEDICATION iv

ACKNOWLEDGEMENTS iii

PREFACE v

LIST OF ABBREVIATIONS

INTRODUCTION -- 1

CHAPTER ONE -- 5
RUPIAH BANDA BECOMES PRESIDENT

CHAPTER TWO -- 15
MY STATE HOUSE APPOINTMENT

CHAPTER THREE -- 21
CHANGING THE SYSTEM

CHAPTER FOUR -- 29
STATE OF THE NATION ADDRESS

CHAPTER FIVE -- 35
THE WORKS OF MY HAND

CHAPTER SIX -- 45
DEALING WITH SCANDALS

CHAPTER SEVEN -- 57
MONKEY URINATES ON THE PRESIDENT

CHAPTER EIGHT -- 71
FOREIGN TRIPS AND DIPLOMACY

CHAPTER NINE -- 83
HELPING THE IVORIANS

CHAPTER TEN -- 89
THE PRESIDENT'S HATCHET MAN

CHAPTER ELEVEN -- 99
"THE COOKIE IS CRUMBLING"

CHAPTER TWELVE -- 109
"WHERE THERE IS HATRED LET ME BRING LOVE"

PICTURES - 117

CHAPTER THIRTEEN -- 141
WORKING WITH A SPORTING PRESIDENT

CHAPTER FOURTEEN -- 151
"A DAMN GOOD PRESIDENT"

CHAPTER FIFTEEN -- 161
A PRESIDENT FOR ALL ZAMBIANS!

CHAPTER SIXTEEN -- 171
CRYING WOLF AHEAD OF VOTING

CHAPTER SEVENTEEN -- 181
STABILITY, SECURITY AND PROSPERITY

CHAPTER EIGHTEEN -- 191
THE LAST MANIFEST

CHAPTER NINETEEN -- 201
DON'T KILL THE MESSENGER

CHAPTER TWENTY -- 209
THE END OF AN ERA

CHAPTER TWENTY-ONE -- 217
THE MISSING GOLD

CHAPTER TWENTY-TWO -- 223
THERE IS LIFE AFTER PRESIDENCY

CHAPTER TWENTY-THREE -- 231
MY REFLECTIONS

LIST OF ABBREVIATIONS

1	ACC	Anti-Corruption Commission
2	AFCON	Africa Cup of Nations
3	AGOA	African Growth and Opportunity Act
4	AFP	Agence France-Presse
5	AU	Africa Union
6	ASA	South America Summit
7	APNAC	The African Parliamentarians Network Against Corruption
8	BBC	British Broadcasting Corporation
9	CENI	Commission Electorale Nationale Indépendante (Independent National Election Commission)
10	CIA	Central Intelligence Agency
11	DEC	Drug Enforcement Commission
12	DBZ	Development Bank of Zambia
13	DRC	Democratic Republic of Congo
14	DPP	Director of Public Prosecution
15	ECZ	Electoral Commission of Zambia
16	ECOWAS	The Economic Community of West African States
17	EISA	Electoral Institute for Sustainable Democracy in Africa
18	FAZ	Football Association of Zambia
19	FAO	Food and Agriculture Organization
20	FIFA	Fédération Internationale de Football Association
21	FRA	Food Reserve Agency
22	FISP	Farmer Input Support Programme
23	ICC	International Criminal Court
24	IOC	International Olympics Committee
25	IJF	International Judo Federation
26	ICGLR	International Conference on the Great Lakes Region
27	IMF	International Monetary Fund
28	JCTR	Jesuit Centre for Theological Reflection
29	LAZ	Law Association of Zambia
30	MISA	Media Institute of Southern Africa
31	MMD	Movement for Multiparty Democracy
32	MP	Member of Parliament
33	NDI	National Democratic Institute
34	NGO	Non Governmental Organization

35	NGOCC	Non Governmental Organization Coordinating Committee
36	NIPA	National Institute of Public Administration
37	NRC	National Registration Card
38	NSCZ	National Sports Council of Zambia
39	OYDC	Olympic Youth Development Centre
40	PF	Patriotic Front
41	PVT	Parallel Voter Tabulation
42	UDPCI	Union for Democracy and Peace in the Ivory Coast
43	UN	United Nations
44	UNIP	United National Independence Party
45	UNDP	United Nations Development Programme
46	UNESCO	United Nations Educational, Scientific and Cultural Organization
47	UPND	United Party for National Development
48	SADC	Southern Africa Development Community
49	TIZ	Transparency International Zambia
50	ZAMTEL	Zambia Telecommunication Corporation
51	ZCCM-IH	Zambia Consolidated Copper Mines – Investment Holdings
52	ZEC	Zambia Episcopal Conference
53	ZESCO	Zambia Electricity Supply Corporation
54	ZNBC	Zambia National Broadcasting Corporation

INTRODUCTION

The President wept, openly.

His wife Thandiwe Chilongo Banda consoled him by placing her hand on his shoulder gently as he reached for a crystal white handkerchief from his pocket to wipe out the tears.

It was September 23, 2011.

President Rupiah Bwezani Banda of Zambia had lost the 2011 presidential election the night before and had called for an urgent early-morning press conference at State House.

Was he going to concede defeat? That was the question on everyone's lips.

He again broke down in the presence of a horde of local and foreign journalists who swarmed State House. Photographers jostled for space to get the best shots of the Head of State and Commander In-Chief of the Armed Forces before what was sure to be a historic moment whichever way.

Apparently, word had gone round that President Banda had called the press conference to dispute the results - as has become common in African states.

I was his spokesman, press advisor and confidant.

I trembled as I called the press conference to order and sung the national anthem.

Key Presidential advisors and senior staff at State House sat behind the President for solidarity. Others wept when he began flipping through the pages of his speech.

I had spent the night before fixing the speech, which was drafted by his British political consultants; Bell Pottinger, a UK communications firm run by Lord Bell, an experienced political strategist who served as Lady Margaret Thatcher's political advisor.

The firm had been hired to assist with the campaign after they had successfully helped Banda win the presidential polls three-years earlier.

The President and I worked throughout that night on the speech, making changes and additions.

Afterwards he went to bed, leaving me to work out the final version for delivery at the much anticipated morning press conference.

The final official results had not been declared even as we finalized the speech. But we had received credible preliminary figures showing that for the president, it was game over! There was still some hope though, and an insistence by some that we should wait until the last ballots had been counted and the result declared-*it was the first past the post-electoral system after all!*

The President's political team insisted, for instance, that their figures showed a clear win for the president. But the President and many in his inner circle knew it was not possible to close the over 100,000-vote gap from the remaining polling stations.

By midnight, the Electoral Commission of Zambia (ECZ) chairperson Justice Irene Mambilima announced the official results - the opposition leader Michael Chilufya Sata of the Patriotic Front (PF) had won the presidential race by a majority of 189,000 votes.

His supporters were ecstatic.

Some marched on the streets in celebration and others attempted to enter State House to force Banda and his family out. But they were blocked as all roads leading to executive mansion were closed.

Armoured vehicles and open vans with heavy artillery on the rooftops patrolled the streets near the Presidential residence.

Some thought the transition would be bloody.

Increased police patrols in the capital Lusaka further amplified speculation that Banda may not concede.

The election had been too close to call until the last votes were in. Some opposition leaders and ministers quietly telephoned the President urging him not to accept the result.

But his inner circle knew that he had already made up his mind and had started packing his personal belongings at Nkhwazi House – the family residence of the Zambian President.

It was the end of an era – the Banda era.

"I have no ill feelings in my heart; there is no malice in my words. Now is the time for me to step aside for a new leader and it is time for me to say goodbye," the 74-year old President said before he broke down again.

That Press Conference was also my last assignment as State House Spokesman and Presidential Advisor.

I had worked with President Banda for the three-years that he served leading Zambia. My initial appointment was as the President's Chief Policy Analyst for Press. He subsequently elevated me to the position of Special Assistant for Press and Public Relations.

In the following chapters, I chronicle my experiences working in State House – from dealing with cabinet ministers, civil servants, diplomats, military and intelligence officers to handling the press and the general public – which was my core job. It was quite an experience. Hard work, infighting, intrigues, and "firefighting" were part of it. At times it was positively exciting and enjoyable.

CHAPTER ONE

RUPIAH BANDA BECOMES PRESIDENT

It was one of the greatest political comebacks in Zambia.

Rupiah Bwezani Banda, who had retired from public life- several years earlier, was now President of the Southern Africa country of Zambia.

It was by a quirk of political fortunes that Mr. Banda became the fourth President and Commander In-Chief of the Armed Forces of the Republic of Zambia. Just a few months before, it was inconceivable that he could end up in the highest office in the land.

He was plucked from retirement and political obscurity by Zambia's third President, Levy Patrick Mwanawasa, who appointed him Zambia's Vice President in 2006. Banda, then 70 years old, had ran his long race of public service and retired quietly to his hometown of Chipata in eastern Zambia close to the Malawian border. He had rapidly exited politics following the death of his first wife, Hope, and up to that point mainly watched Zambian developments from sidelines. The country had forgotten about him. Very few young people remembered or even knew much about him.

To many, he was largely yesterday's man.

He had served as Minister of Foreign Affairs in the administration of Zambia's first and founding President, Dr. Kenneth Kaunda.

He served in other capacities too, including that of Ambassador to the United Nations, the United States of America, and Egypt. In addition he had held roles of Minister of State for Mines, Governor of the capital, Lusaka, as well as Chief Executive Officer of two big state-owned agricultural companies.

Banda, like many of his contemporaries left active politics to pave way for a younger generation of politicians in 1991. This is .after President Kaunda lost the presidency in the historic 1991 multiparty elections, which ended his 27 years at the helm. The elections marked the return of plural politics to Zambia after 17 years of one-party rule.

"I am a political dinosaur," Banda liked to joke while President.

Two years after he was made Vice-President, Banda was thrust to the helm of leadership in the country following tragic circumstances. This was after the collapse of President Mwanawasa in Egypt while attending an African Union summit. The President was never to regain consciousness.

By virtue of being the Vice President, Banda was the constitutional successor and immediately took over as acting President. This would last for 90 days until a presidential by-election was held, according to the constitution.

Some of his colleagues in government wanted him to leave the stage for a younger person. But many more encouraged him to run for the top office.

My involvement in his presidential campaign was by accident.

I received a telephone call from Mbita Chitala, a founding member of the ruling Movement for Multiparty Democracy (MMD) party. He sounded furious on the phone and wanted to meet me urgently.

He wanted me to help him draft a statement endorsing acting President Banda for President in the forthcoming by-election.

He had been worked up by a radio report that day that another politician and former cabinet minister Dipak Patel had endorsed Finance Minister Ng'andu Magande for president.

"I want you to help me do a good statement."

It was around 12:30 hours.

I suggested to him that the statement goes on FM Radio Phoenix, which had a wide listenership. The station had its main news bulletin at 13:00 hours. If we had to work on a written statement, I told him, it would not make it to the bulletin. It would be too late.

I immediately dialed the station's news editor then, Julius Sakala, a schoolmate and requested coverage for Chitala.

The station interviewed him live on the main news.

Chitala attacked those who he said had breached Zambian cultural norms by openly talking about succession before the deceased President was buried. He ended by endorsing acting President Rupiah Banda saying Banda had demonstrated impeccable leadership qualities during the sickness and eventual death of Mwanawasa.

"Rupiah Banda has held the country together during these trying moments," Chitala said.

******

A total of 15 candidates had filed their applications when the party opened nominations for the presidential candidate.

Banda was the front-runner but was facing a strong challenge from Finance Minister Magande. Among the other candidates were Home Affairs Minister, Lt-General Ronnie Shikapwasha, Health Minister Brian Chituwo and the respected lawyer and former President of the African Development Bank (AfDB), Willa Mung'omba.

Also in the running was the renowned tele-evangelist Nevers Mumba who had once served as Mwanawasa's Vice-President.

Banda had an inbuilt majority in the Electoral College going by the public endorsements he received. Almost all party provincial conferences had thrown their weight behind him and the battle was clearly between Banda and Magande.

The independent private daily, *The Post,* intensified the campaign for Magande and went negative on Banda. At that time, I was editing an online intelligence-based publication called *Executive Issues*, which provided some relief for the Banda team.

By the time the party went to the polls on September 5, 2008, the Magande campaign had run out of steam and it was clear that Banda would get it. There were, however, still attempts at political horse-trading.

A number of suggestions were floated such as talking some candidates out of the race. There were also attempts to persuade Banda to appoint Magande Vice-President if the latter withdrew from the race.

Banda declined and instead insisted on the polls going ahead with the full field.

"I don't want to discourage anyone from standing. It is democracy, they are free to contest," he said.

******

September 5, 2008 was balloting day.

The election took place at the Mulungushi International Conference Centre in Lusaka.

A carnival atmosphere characterized the voting process as scores of Banda supporters converged outside the meeting hall waving pro-Banda placards. They sang and danced as they waited for the counting to end and the declaration of the result.

Banda was the runaway winner with 47 votes against 11 for Magande. The rest of the candidates did very badly.

It was now official. Banda was the presidential candidate of the governing MMD in the forthcoming presidential by-election.

The following day, Banda met with the MMD's financial committee to discuss the financial state of the party in view of the campaign ahead. The news was discouraging. The party was in the red! Broke!

"I prayed to God and asked why he had made me a candidate yet I had no money to campaign," Banda would later say publicly.

******

The campaign was soon underway in earnest.

His main opponent, Michael Chilufya Sata of the Patriotic Front was already ahead working the ground. He had started while the MMD squabbled over who their candidate would be.

After Magande had been routed, the *Post* threw its weight behind Sata, who looked unstoppable with his brand of populism.

Sata has charisma and is a natural dramatist whose oratory holds audiences.

"Within 90 days, I will transform Zambia," Sata would tell the urban poor disenchanted with the liberal-economic policies of the MMD.

He had the other advantage of having been in the presidential race twice before. This was his third time and many voters naturally knew him well.

Banda, on the other hand, was largely unknown to the younger generation. His opponents further created the impression that Banda was a mere villager plucked from a farm in Chipata by Mwanawasa to become Vice President.

The Post tried to portray Banda's campaign rallies as flops attended mainly by small children while Sata's rallies were portrayed as crowd-pullers.

The Banda campaign got off to a sluggish start and appeared to lack any real momentum.

A rashly set up Campaign Center failed to coordinate well.

For instance, there were up to four media teams working for Banda or "RB", each working independently with little coordination between them.

It was when I worked on the campaign website after he became acting President that I personally got to talk to Banda in detail for the first time.

I was frank with him on a number of issues affecting his campaign.

Most of those who visited him at Government House, the official residence of the Vice-President, told him only what he wanted to hear.

He liked my candidness.

"*Baba* I have no one to help me handle the press, I hope you will assist me when I need you here," Banda told me after I coordinated a series of his interviews with the foreign press.

I also organized wide-ranging interviews with Frank Mutubila, a veteran broadcaster, which improved RB's image and visibility when they were broadcast. Banda came out very crispy in television interviews better than his opponents.

And that is how I became part of his team.

But overall, Banda's showing in the campaign was still a source of concern.

Most members of the party were hesitant to campaign for him openly because they saw him as an outsider as he had not been a member of the party for long.

To make matters worse, the Members of Parliament were not seeking a fresh mandate and so they had limited incentive to campaign for the president.

RB toured all the nine provinces, holding a series of election rallies in a compressed schedule as the campaign period was only four weeks.

As the campaign progressed, so did the dynamics and the competition landscape. Edith Nawakwi, Sakwiba Sikota and Benjamin Mwila, notable opposition leaders, withdrew from the race and declared for Banda.

The feeling among discerning supporters and sympathizers came to be that he needed to urgently improve his ratings before polling day - October 30, 2008.

The British Firm – Bell Pottinger – was hired to help with the public relations as well as political strategy in that short window before the elections.

This did not go down well with some senior party members who were skeptical about engaging foreigners, arguing that foreigners could not be in a position to tell seasoned local politicians how to win an election in Zambia.

So, the 'Team' as we called them, faced massive opposition starting from the party rank and file to the Campaign Center. But Rupiah Banda, with his vast international experience, knew well that he needed the firm.

Most candidates worldwide rely on such firms for unbiased insights. Banda gave the 'Team' all the protection and support.

Initially, he had appointed lawyer Henry Mbushi to coordinate the Team's work.

I was to replace him in that role as the campaign progressed.

We used to meet almost every day at Government House in the famous 'Blue Room', where we could coach the acting President. It was a very small and carefully selected group – no one knew about it initially. I was one of about six to seven close-knit group of the acting President that met in the evenings to hatch out plans.

Bell Pottinger is an international public relations firm with vast experience in electioneering. They have advised on elections in a number of countries, Zambia being one of them.

They set up camp at Binnie Lodge in Lusaka's Kabulonga area. They devised a quick campaign strategy after conducting a countrywide opinion poll that showed Banda trailing. One of the main weaknesses of the Banda campaign, the poll revealed, was a lack of a coordinated interface with the press. A plan of action was devised and put in action.

Polling went smoothly on Election Day October 30 and everyone was now anxious for the result.

The Electoral Commission of Zambia (ECZ) had established an election results center at the Mulungushi International Conference Centre from where the public was routinely updated with the latest figures.

******

The election night was one of the longest I have had to endure in my life.

James Banda, the eldest son of Rupiah Banda, was my regular contact during that period. We were like Siamese twins and were constantly in each other's company.

'The old man' had summoned James and I to join him at Government House as he anxiously awaited the results.

It was a full house when we got there. Close friends and relatives were all seated in the Blue Room with Banda. They had pen and paper and jotted down every result coming in from our agents posted across the country.

James and I didn't like the pervasive tense atmosphere in the room.

"My brother lets go in the field and get the results," James beckoned to me as he apologized to his father that we needed to leave.

We immediately drove to Johnny's, a Chinese Restaurant and Bar in Lagos Road in Rhodespark, Lusaka, where we had set up base for refreshments. There, at least, the atmosphere was jovial and light. Everyone was convinced, including waiters, that we had won the polls.

The following day, the last results trickled in but still the opposition candidate had a lead. However, the tally from our agents across the country still indicated that we had won by over 50,000 votes. We in the inner circle had that figure.

I was relaxed during the wait knowing very well that it was a matter of time before the champagne would flow.

Something dramatic and quite extraordinary thing happened just before the official results were released. Some senior members of the Banda campaign team approached him to concede defeat to Sata. He was shocked and refused to heed!

After a long wait, ECZ chairperson Justice Florence Mumba officially announced the results and, as expected, declared Banda duly elected President of the Republic of Zambia with slightly over 58,000 more votes than his closest challenger Michael Sata of the PF.

I was happy that I had fully participated in the making of a head of state. My previous forays, working with presidential candidates - Dean Mung'omba in 1996 and Anderson Mazoka in 2001 – had been unsuccessful. But here I was, seated in a huge marquee, with high-level VIPs, witnessing the man I worked for during the campaign, taking the oath of the highest office in Zambia.

A swearing-in ceremony was organized within 24 hours as provided for by the Constitution.

Foreign dignitaries and Heads of State arrived in the morning to attend the inauguration of Zambia's fourth President at the Parliament Buildings on November 2, 2008.

It was carnival time.

The President-elect arrived in a black metallic, bullet-proof Mercedes Benz car and inspected a guard of honour mounted by the Lusaka-based second battalion Zambia regiment.

There was a 21 gun-salute followed by a fly past by three fighter jets of the Zambia Air Force.

An immaculately dressed Banda walked alongside his wife, now First Lady, Thandiwe Chilongo, as he waved to the cheering crowd.

As he began reading the Oath of Office:

"I, Rupiah Bwezani Banda, having been elected President of the Republic of Zambia, I do hereby..." his voice was muffled by loud cheers from the crowd as he completed the reading the rest of the Oath of Office.

A presidential salute was performed as the national anthem played in the background. Banda left the podium to the waiting Presidential motorcade on his first drive as President of Zambia surrounded by smartly-dressed out-riders in white and blue police uniform on BMW motorcycles.

The anxiety was over! He was the president!

A luncheon followed at Government House for the visiting dignitaries.

I quickly rushed there. I had not bothered to get an official invitation card – for what? I thought, I was part of the team and no one could stop me.

Arriving at Government House I found changes. Heavily armed presidential guards now patrolled the perimeter. Our usual security people from the campaign who knew me were nowhere in sight. The state security detail for the President had taken over and firmly.

Some of Banda's close relatives were barred from entering the premises as the new guard took charge.

I approached the gate but the unfriendly and uncompromising officers refused to allow me in. I used to drive in and out every day but now things had clearly changed.

I called William Banda, a politician, who had made himself Private Secretary to the acting President during the campaign. He could not help. He was equally 'chased' from Government House. There could now be no doubt that State House staff had taken over the show for sure. It took the intervention of the president's Aide De Camp to "rescue me."

We had a good lunch in the scorching heat on the lawns of Government House. When I tried to reach the old man, I was almost manhandled by the security that maintained a ring around him, even at a luncheon. It took his intervention for them allow me through.

"*Anyamata, ni mwana wanga uyo*...[young men he is my son]" Banda shouted from his table.

The officers didn't see that the President had signaled me to walk to his table.

From that day, I vowed to stay away unless the President called me. The next day, the President organized a dinner for the 'Team', the Bell Pottinger group that had played a key role in his victory and I was asked to attend.

He thanked everyone who participated and made his victory possible.

******

Soon I was back at my usual job, editing *Executive Issues* and doing some work for Agence France Presse (AFP) although I had informed the French during the campaign that I wanted to quit. The Bureau Chief for Southern Africa had declined my resignation and asked me to think it over. I was also doing some work on political profiling under my firm, Brentwood Public Affairs Limited. I had literally switched off from politics. After all, my assistance in the campaign was separate from me looking for a job. I had participated in the campaign because I believed in the candidate.

Two weeks after President Banda took office, I received an early morning telephone call from State House.

"The President wants to see you," the caller who identified himself as a senior private secretary to the President said.

When I got to State House that morning, I discovered that I was overdressed for the meeting. The President was in a pair of shorts, walking shoes and a golf T-shirt.

I was in a navy-blue pinstriped suit, white shirt and polka-dotted red necktie and a matching pocket-handkerchief.

"They didn't tell you I wanted you to join me for a walk?" Banda asked as he emerged from a thicket on the State House golf course.

In tow were dozens of plain-clothed bodyguards walking beside him.

We sat in the gardens, admiring blooming flowers, as we chatted over a number of issues concerning the country.

The President said he was happy with the way I had coordinated his media team and would like us to work together, that is if I was willing to be part of his State House senior advisory staff.

Banda was selecting his team at State House.

"When do you start work?" he asked as we parted.

I never expected the question.

"When I receive the letter sir," I answered as he escorted me to my car.

CHAPTER TWO
MY STATE HOUSE APPOINTMENT

A month passed without receiving my appointment letter.

I had submitted my updated Curriculum Vitae to the Cabinet Office, the headquarters of government administration in Zambia and done the requisite medicals.

The President telephoned me again.

"When are you reporting for work?" he asked.

"I have not received the letter sir," I politely responded.

"Please come for work tomorrow. Nobody will stop you. I am your letter," he said.

"This is the kind of bureaucracy in the civil service that we need to change," he said before ending the call.

He sounded upset with the delay in formalizing my appointment and I began to feel a personal bond with him.

The security people, I was told, were still doing background checks on me. A clean criminal record is a requirement for appointment to a State House post.

But I had been arrested twice in two years in connection with two serious security offences.

I was implicated in the failed military coup of 1997 and two years later was picked up on espionage charges.

Even though I was acquitted on spying charges by the High Court and was never prosecuted for treason, the records remained.

Against that background I suspected that a clean security bill of health was going to be problematic.

That, I knew and I believe the President too had an idea.

As a reporter, I had had a fair share of brushes with the authorities.

In 1999, I was among the twelve journalists from the independent daily, *The Post*, who were rounded up and charged with espionage following a report in the newspaper that discussed Zambia's military capabilities compared to Angola. It was at a time of worsening animosity between the two neighbouring countries over the civil war in that country.

We were accused of spying for Angola against our own country.

After a lengthy trial in the Lusaka High Court, we were all acquitted.

Similarly, in 1997, I was picked up in connection with a story that I wrote that predicted "an explosion" and was published a day before the failed military coup of October 1997 that was staged by junior army officers. The story quoted Zambia's founding President Kenneth Kaunda predicting that "something big will happen" on the eve of the putsch.

Kaunda was subsequently arrested and detained based on my story.

I was under investigation for "misprision" or concealing treason. No formal charge was preferred and I was released after interrogations. This was after I had gone "underground" for close to six-months to elude the police.

I was also among the "banned persons" prohibited from entering any military base in Zambia. I, together with two other reporters, were put on that list after we were arrested and briefly detained at the Zambia Air Force base in Lusaka for allegedly taking photographs of military installations without authority. Our camera was confiscated.

Despite this background, my clearance to work at State House which came through showed that I was not exactly in bad books with the authorities.

The late President Levy Mwanawasa had appointed me a commissioner on the 41-member Constitution Review Commission that was to draft the new Zambian constitution.

I had by then left the controversial newspaper, *The Post* and was a freelance journalist.

I took up a weekly column with *The Monitor* newspaper while stringing for a number of foreign publications such as *Africa Confidential, Africa Energy, Radio France International, BBC Africa Service, Africa Eye News Agency, Agence France Presse (AFP)* and many more. I found working as a freelance journalist very exciting.

The French News agency AFP offered me a steady job which made me travel around the African continent and work in the Johannesburg and Nairobi bureaus, with frequent stints at the head office in Paris.

My work was widely published around the world and I became a political commentator on African Affairs, frequently featuring as a guest speaker on South Africa's talk show radio – *Radio 702*.

So I had a good understanding of both the local and international press by the time I was appointed to State House.

I knew the challenges, which reporters faced in Africa, especially in accessing information from the normally reticent government officials.

Many colleagues were happy with my appointment and expected a change in the way State House handled media issues. The President had picked one of them.

"You are our ambassador in State House because you know our problems," one colleague said in a private note.

Even people outside the media welcomed my appointment.

"I have always had tremendous respect and admiration for your mature, professional skills and disposition. It did not surprise me to learn that the President saw it fit to appoint you as his head of media relations at State House," read a letter from Patrick Chisanga, a respected Rotarian and businessman.

"You have done us proud. You have over the years ably demonstrated your professionalism as one of Zambia's leading journalists. And nobody can doubt that," said Professor Kenneth Mwenda of the World Bank in Washington.

My parents were excited with news of my appointment.

"This is the big appointment my son. Please, please, serve the President with all the loyalty and honesty," was a line of advice from my father, Dickson Jere Sr.

For my mother, Mary Banda Jere, it was a long ululation and a word of encouragement.

"Always remember to pray to God everyday morning," she said.

Outside the media mainstream, I also had the background of having worked with a number of civil society organizations. In 2002, I was elected chairman of the Zambian Chapter of the Media Institute of Southern Africa (MISA). I was also board member of the Media Trust Fund, Media Law Reforms Committee and the MISA regional governing council. I sat on the board of the Citizens Forum, a pro-democracy NGO.

I worked as a media consultant for the European Union Electoral Observation Mission to Zambia, as well as for the Canadian Mission in Lusaka and Malawi.

I was also a lead consultant in the setting up of the Public Relations Wing of the Zambian Judiciary under the Access to Justice Project of the Ministry of Justice.

My journalism skills began during my high school days at Munali Boys Secondary School in Lusaka where I edited a school newspaper, the '*Munali News*', and was a key member of the writers club.

I am a trained journalist, having graduated from the Evelyn Hone College of Applied Arts and Commerce with a Diploma in Journalism and Public Relations.

I later underwent post-graduate training in Radio Production at the CIFAP Institute in Paris, France and attended an Investigative Reporting Course at the Institute for the Advancement of Journalism in South Africa. I also attended a number of other professional courses on various aspects of journalism and reporting.

I hold a Bachelor's Degree in Law (LLB) from the University of Zambia. My State House appointment prevented me from taking the bar examinations to be admitted as an advocate of the Judicature for Zambia. Since leaving State House I prioritized taking the bar exam which I eventually passed and was officially called to the bar on March 14, 2014.

I had in the past quietly worked with two unsuccessful presidential candidates. I was in the team of the late Dean Mung'omba in 1996 and worked with the late Anderson Mazoka in 2001. In 2006, I was one of the people who attended the first in a series of meetings that brokered an alliance between Michael Sata's Patriotic Front (PF) and the smaller United Liberal Party (ULP). With two parties behind him, Sata narrowly lost the presidency in that election.

So, I had considerable political experience at the relatively young age of 32 years when I was appointed to serve in the Banda administration.

On the morning I reported for work at State House, there was panic.

I had not taken the Oath of office and Allegiance, which entailed being bound to secrecy before I could access confidential State House files and offices. So, without receiving a formal appointment letter, a rashly organized swearing-in ceremony was set for the afternoon.

It was a solemn occasion – everyone in attendance was required to dress in dark somber colours.

At exactly 14:00 hours, I was seated, with three other new appointees, in the Cabinet Room, in readiness for the ceremony. I was dressed in a dark blue two-buttoned suit, navy blue shirt with a dark blue polka dot necktie and a matching handkerchief hanging on the top pocket of my jacket.

Three other appointees, the political advisor Akashambatwa Mbikusita-Lewanika, lawyer Anne Sitali who had just been appointed Permanent Secretary for the Ministry of Justice and Davies Sampa, Permanent Secretary in the Office of the Vice President were also due to be sworn in.

Some cabinet ministers, top civil servants and State House staff were all in attendance, waiting for the President to begin the ceremony.

The function always begins with a rendition of the national anthem.

With a raised Bible in my right hand and Oath form in my left, I recited the oath:

"I, Dickson Jere, having been appointed Chief Analyst for Press and Public Relations at State House, do hereby, solemnly swear...." I read the Oath of Allegiance to the President as he stood opposite me, looking directly into my eyes.

I shivered a bit before regaining composure.

He was dressed in a dark blue suit and white shirt. He looked somewhat different from the man I had been interacting with.

I could feel the aura of authority around him.

Flashes of light from cameras were focused on me from a band of photographers who had come to cover the function. I knew literally everyone since I had worked with them for years. It was a solemn occasion not least because it marked the end of my career as a journalist at least to the immediate future and I had cherished it.

I was now officially a State House insider.

Later on the President completed his team, which included me in charge of Press and Public Relations although I ended up doing many other assignments outside my portfolio. I was promoted from Chief Policy Analyst to Special Assistant to the President on April 22, 2009, just after four months in the job.

The Chief of Staff was an academician Dr. Austin Sichinga, the Economic Advisor was Dr. Richard Chembe who was appointed from the Central Bank while Joseph Jalasi was the Legal advisor.

Other presidential assistants were the former Agriculture Minister Benedict Kapita who was in charge of Project Monitoring and Implementation. Another former Minister Mbikusita-Lewanika was Political advisor and was later replaced by the academician Dr. Francis Chigunta from the University of Zambia. The Chief of Protocol was Bob Samakai who was transferred from Foreign Affairs to State House.

Apart from Chembe, I had dealt with the rest of the team on different occasions before we all met at State House. So they all were familiar.

We all had our assistants working under the title of Chief Policy Analyst while the advisors were called Special Assistants to the President or 'Specials' as we were commonly known in government circles.

The head of the Presidential security detail was Charles Kaonga from Zambia Police (Special Duties) and the President's personal physician was Dr. Shaileni Desai. The Aide De Camp to the President was Steven Mayoko.

That was the full complement of the Banda team that was to work with him during the three-year tenure.

CHAPTER THREE
CHANGING THE SYSTEM

My first official trip with the President was on December 13, 2008.

At 07:00 hours, the propeller engines of the Zambian version of *Air Force "One"* – the presidential plane -were revving noisily at the City Airport Air force base located a few meters from State House.

The smartly dressed crew of the Chinese-made MA60 aircraft commanded by Air force Colonel Muliokela Muliokela stood at the door, guard-of-honour style.

They wore smartly pressed navy blue shirts, grey trousers and navy blue berets.

President Banda, dressed in a grey suit without a necktie, alighted from his black Mercedes Benz limousine as all uniformed officers stood still and saluted.

We were going to Luanshya, a small copper mining town, where the copper mine faced a bleak future. The owners of the mine had said that they had no alternative but to close it down in view of the global recession and financial crisis of 2008 that led to a near-collapse of the copper prices.

Hundreds of workers would lose their livelihood. Barely a month in office, President Banda decided to travel there and discuss the impending lay-offs with the miners and the management.

Such boldness and directness were to be the hallmark of his time in office.

We were airborne within minutes.

I sat next to him as he explained to me his strategy for approaching the angry and dispirited miners. The security had warned against the trip because it rated the risk of trouble high.

"The Chinese are willing to buy off these mines and keep the jobs." he hinted.

After nearly one hour in the air, we landed at Simon Mwansa Kapwepwe International Airport in Ndola and immediately boarded the waiting vehicles for the 45 minute-drive to Luanshya.

With sirens from the police vehicles, we were on the Ndola-Kitwe dual carriageway and the vehicle in which I rode was almost at the tail end of the motorcade.

Behind our car was an open white Toyota Land cruiser van, which carried heavily armed presidential guards.

The motorcade was quick but still created a traffic jam in the city.

There were armed policemen at intervals along the route in what is known as 'route lining' as I was to learn later.

Children and other onlookers had lined up the route to try and catch a glimpse of the president.

I have never been a fan of presidential motorcades especially when roads are closed to other users. I had been a victim of such closures before. It wasn't pleasant. This time, however, I was part of the motorcade I previously never appreciated.

I thought the police exaggerated the security around the president. It now struck me that I would have to try and change that.

The political strategists during the election campaign also detested the security people for their tendency to drive a wedge between the candidate and the voters. Now I thought I had the opportunity to bring change to this tradition. After all, I was in charge of the President's public relations and I thought my job description allowed me to suggest the change.

It was not to be! My efforts only attracted some straight talking:

"Mr. Jere, you found us here and you will leave us here. Just concentrate on doing speeches and press releases," I was told by the security people.

"Leave issues of security to security and we shall also leave press matters to the press," they said before patting me on the back saying I was welcome to the 'system'.

The 'system' referred to the entire State House bureaucracy and associated security apparatus for the country.

******

The meeting with miners in Luanshya was heated.

But the President's gift of combining serious discussions with a sense of humor was a source of strength to his staff.

"I will not allow this mine to close," he said.

The angry and dispirited miners cheered.

He said mining investors who felt they would have to close should hand the mines over to the government through the state mining investment company, ZCCM-IH so that new investors could be found.

The Chinese were willing buyers, they had the money and Zambia made no secret of the fact that they would not hesitate to sell to willing buyers.

It was an approach that was to save the country mass unemployment.

Seemingly, unwilling to sell to the Chinese, the mainly western interests that owned them were forced to revise their plans and to keep the mines running. Only two closed during that recession.

******

We arrived back in the capital by the early evening.

The next morning, I was shown my office. It was clear that I would need new office equipment- PC, fax machine and telephone handsets. Internet connectivity in my office would need a boost.

I had a quiet discussion with the head of administration over the state of equipment in my office. He was apologetic but not about to change anything!

I moved my personal laptop computer to the office, connected it to the Internet and got the printer fixed.

There was no budget line for the department.

That is how I began work. I was in a hurry to make a difference.

"You need to get your assistants quickly," the President said after noticing that work was piling up on my desk because in addition to my portfolio I did other work for him.

Journalists Charles Kachikoti as my deputy and Kennedy Limwanya as press officer later joined me.

State House had no official photographer. I immediately put in a request and got the swift response that it required treasury approval from the Ministry of Finance.

Damn!

Will I succeed to change anything here? I sighed.

From my quick online check with other African State Houses, I realized my department was completely understaffed. It was made up of only the three of us!

State House in the smaller country of Burundi in East Africa, for instance, had over ten staff to run the Presidential press and public relations unit.

I wanted to have a person specifically for monitoring the mushrooming FM radio stations and find ways of responding on a daily basis if necessary. I also wanted a person to monitor television as well as one for scanning and blogging on the various online publications.

I couldn't get any!

I needed a fax machine in order for State House statements to reach all rural-based radio stations that had no internet connection.

"No sir, there is a department, which is responsible for all outgoing faxes from State House. Here, we are not allowed to send any mail," my secretary told me.

"Why?" I enquired.

"It's for security reasons. They need to have details of all outgoing mail from here," she said.

I now realized that I needed to work differently to achieve any change at all in the face of several security barriers and civil service red tape.

Presidential speeches and State House press statements had hitherto been sent only to the state-run media.

I decided to change that to the annoyance of the 'system'. I created a mailing list of almost all journalists in Zambia and the Southern African region.

While the old guards at State House were not titillated, my press colleagues were happy.

"The press releases are helpful. I don't remember a time when we had a press secretary send us Press Releases through Internet. It's a break through...," read an email from Father Freeborn Kibombwe, a Roman Catholic priest who ran a community radio station in western Zambia.

A foreign correspondent, Michael Malakata, e-mailed me on December 26, 2008:

"It gives us pleasure as journalists that we have a representative at State House. You have changed the wrong thinking that ZNBC, Daily Mail, Times and the Post are the only media."

The Media Institute of Southern Africa (MISA) through its chairperson Henry Kabwe also appreciated the changes I implemented.

"From the look of things, it appears that you still espouse the values of easy access to information and press freedom. I have noted with gladness trends that are currently prevailing with your guidance."

I was encouraged by the feedback.

Using my newswire skills, I developed a template for news releases written in a story form for radio stations. I realized that most of community radio stations had no capacity to digest an over 50-page speech and write a story. So, we decided to do their job by summarizing each speech.

It worked well.

Most radio stations read the State House statements in full.

I set my next stop for the State House Website.

I pulled it down in short order.

It still described the events around the late president, had his picture and speeches nearly four months after his death. The basic data was not of much use to researchers on the presidency.

I subcontracted a private web-designer to re-do the site and make it interactive. My plan was to enable people send emails to the President and interact with him on a daily basis.

But I had stepped on some toes by then without realizing it.

Management of the site was outside my responsibility. It was managed by the security people to avoid 'criminals and terrorists' engaging the Head of State.

I was summoned to a high-level meeting where my 'unbecoming' behaviour was on the agenda. I was told of an incident during the tenure of second President Frederick Chiluba when the State House website was hacked and the presidential portrait was replaced with a cartoon by the hackers!

The incident embarrassed the 'system' and that is how the decision was made for the website to be managed by the security people.

"We just need to get an IT guy who can put more security features on the website," I told the meeting.

However, I realized most of the people who were talking didn't have any real knowledge or understanding of the issue.

I began to think that I may have been too fast with my envisioned changes.

The following month, an initiation ceremony into how State House works was arranged for the newly appointed senior staff. We needed to know the 'Dos' and the 'Don'ts'.

We had to go through a crash course in public service management at the National Institute of Public Administration (NIPA).

Veteran bureaucrats were brought to lecture us on how the civil service system operates.

I found the lectures both refreshing and instructive of the operational difficulties faced by the civil service.

"The system checks itself. If you follow the laid down procedures, you won't have problems," one of the tutors said.

"It is the same system that will save you at the crucial moment."

The only problem I had with the bureaucracy was that it was repetitive and did not easily embrace change or new technologies.

Every communication for instance, had to be recorded in a logbook.

"So how should we deal with emails?" I asked.

"My advice is avoid email communication," was the answer.

I never heeded that advice as I used email communication extensively and effectively especially when dealing with other press aides from different countries.

During a visit to Rwanda it became clear that the civil service there had embraced the new technologies that were working perfectly. This was in contrast with my country Zambia.

Our next initiation was into the intelligence business.

It was one of the most interesting training and interaction with an organization that remains largely shadowy. One that is at once intriguing and mysterious.

During our initiation, I came to appreciate its role as important in order to assure national security. Contrary to some negative perceptions, intelligence gathering and analysis service helps the Presidency and the government to work smoothly.

"Why don't you open up to the public on some of your work?" I asked acting naïve.

"No, we can't!" was the curt answer and there was no further explanation.

I had argued that even the Central Intelligence Agency (CIA) in the United States and the M16 in Britain had steadily relaxed secrecy and now had even official spokespersons.

Other security wings in Zambia such as the army, air force and police have adapted to new approaches and established public relations offices to interact with the media and citizens but not the Zambia Intelligence Security Services.

Overall, the training was an eye-opener and we learnt a lot!

The last initiation was optional.

It was with Zambia Police (Special Division), which is responsible for presidential guard duties.

Naturally, our work involved constant interaction with the bodyguards and it was prudent that we understood their mission.

Only two took it up - the Chief of State Protocol Bob Samakai and I. It involved handling firearms.

We were trained in dismantling and assembling various weapons within specific times. It was an interesting occupation, which has since become my hobby.

Every Saturday, when time allowed, it was spent at the rifle range.

I perfected shooting skills in handguns and automatic weapons such as the AK47 rifle.

I enjoyed shooting!

I had the last initiation with the President himself. I am not aware whether all my friends went through the same process with the boss.

******

After a few days in State House, the President called for me to his office.

"I have just realized I have not welcomed you properly," he said, sounding very serious.

"Whatever we are going to do together here, it is for the State. No one should know, not even my children," he said.

He gave me a short lecture on the need to separate national from personal issues even with close friends and relatives.

"This is important. You are no longer a free person like before," he said while assuring me of all the support during my time in State House.

Having gone through the initiation ceremonies, I was now a fully-fledged civil servant as well as presidential operative. But that notwithstanding, my urge for reforms did not wane.

There were things that just needed to change.

President Banda was also for change in certain things. That made my work easier as I had the boss for an ally.

He for instance continued to frequent Chinese restaurants in Lusaka and mingle easily with other diners whenever he had an opportunity despite strong objections from his security detail.

Sometimes he even ordered takeaways of his favorite Chinese dishes at State House, a practice that hardly pleased the security people.

On one occasion, the President threatened to drive himself out of State House for lunch at a friend's house. The security detail tried to block his movements saying it was not allowed for the Head of State to eat at private homes without security clearance.

"I will go on my own," he said before the security quickly arranged vehicles to take him for the lunch appointment.

He had wanted to maintain his normal life while in State House.

The President also relaxed the dress code.

During the training, we had been told, without exception, that we were required to be in dark suits throughout. And a necktie was a must! Be it in the bush or not, only the President could dress down but not his staff.

"Why are you wearing suits in the villages? Please remove them," President Banda would issue an order after noticing us struggling in the scorching heat.

He allowed us to wear casual African shirts especially when we were touring the countryside.

Our relaxed dress code did not please the system.

"We were lowering standards around the Presidency," we were told.

A colleague reminded me of Robert Greene's bestseller book, *48 Laws of Power* and in particular Law number 45, which is:

"Preach the need for change, BUT never reform too much at once".

With that law in mind, I decided to slow down. I was converted!

CHAPTER FOUR
STATE OF THE NATION ADDRESS

A 220-page document landed on my desk.

"It's a draft speech for the President, sir," my secretary informed me.

President Banda was due to give his first State of the Nation Address on January 16, 2009. The address, as per tradition, coincided with the official opening of a new session of the National Assembly.

The bound draft speech came from the Cabinet Office. I looked at it so that I could work out a final version due in three days. It was voluminous! I needed to work with speed in order to effectively make the deadline.

I quickly perused through. It was a hodgepodge.

"Don't make changes to the format," my secretary relayed the instructions.

There was a standard template, which every President had to adopt for the state of the nation speech.

Several committees of technocrats and senior civil servants from different departments participated in drafting it. Each of the 20 ministries had to contribute a chapter. However, in its draft form, the speech was just too long!

I knew it would be too much for the President to effectively deliver a 220-page speech in the time allocated.

I sent a copy to him for his input while I settled in my chair for what were to be long hours of putting the text right.

Within minutes, my red line buzzed. The red telephone was the one-way communication channel with the President.

"What is this?" he asked before he burst into loud laughter.

We had been informed that the draft speech delayed because the committee of technocrats had retreated to work out the speech before handing it over to State House.

"I can't deliver such a speech! Please stop whatever you are doing and write a new one," the President said.

"They never even asked me what I wanted to be in that speech," he said.

State House had no speechwriter and such assignments always landed on my desk or that of the Chief of Staff.

"I want a brief speech, straight to the point like the ones during campaign," the President said.

He didn't want it to be more than 30 minutes in duration.

"People get bored with long speeches..." he said.

I used to double-space the President's speech and every word was in capital letters to make them easy to read. The 220 pages would be doubled if I formatted it that way.

By evening, the President had convened a meeting of senior staff. We needed to put our heads together to come up with a new version of the speech.

"Forget about this template. We are going to introduce our own style," the President, in upbeat tone, said.

We worked with him through the night. He went through the new speech page-by-page until we were done by 01:00 hours.

The role of my colleagues was over. The speech was now my baby.

I was back in the office, by 11:00 hours.

The President and I locked ourselves up in an 'interview room' andI took the podium as a dummy President.

I read the speech while he sat and followed attentively.

Occasionally, he would interject to correct the pronunciation. He was good at it.

After he was comfortable with the flow he took the podium himself.

There followed hectic long hours of rehearsal.

No telephone calls or any disturbances were allowed unless it was something of extreme urgency.

I had a stop watch to time his delivery and flow. We had agreed that the speech would be 45 minutes long after the Speaker of the National Assembly had advised that a 30-minutes speech would be too short for the occasion.

President Banda was a very patient man. He paid minute attention to whatever he did and believed in perfection.

"*Baba*, we are not leaving this room until the speech is perfect," he said when he noticed some mistakes in the text.

He read the speech several times until he was comfortable with it.

It was through such moments that I bonded closely with him.

During short breaks, we sat over a cup of tea and scones while chatting about national issues.

There was never a dull moment with President Banda. He was always full of humor and kept me laughing throughout such sessions.

I had wanted him to use the teleprompter in parliament but he had poor eyesight for such technology. So, we had to do with a hardcopy.

By evening we were done with the speech.

"Don't forget to wear a dark suit tomorrow," I told the President as we parted.

It was part of my responsibility to ensure that the President was in correct attire for such occasions. Sometimes, I would call his valet to alert him about the specific dress code for the day.

******

Friday, January 16, 2009 was the state opening of parliament, an occasion characterized by pomp and ceremony.

Traditional dancers bussed from across the country were performing on the lawns of the parliament buildings.

The police brass band played as they awaited the arrival of the President and Commander-in-Chief for his first state of the nation address.

The second battalion of the Zambia regiment mounted a full guard of honour for the President, who arrived in a car ceremonially escorted by mounted police. He wore a navy-blue pinstripe suit, white shirt and blue necktie.

The 21-gun salute rumbled outside the parliament buildings while Zambia Air Force fighter jets flew overhead in a fly past.

I was already in position inside the National Assembly preoccupied with the speech. **It** was my very first speech written for the president. I wanted it to be a success and had a copy to monitor the flow.

The 158 members of parliament were seated, noisily, waiting for the President's speech.

"Order, order, order..." the Speaker, dressed in a red gown and whitish wig, said as he called the House to order.

The President was announced, entered and took his position in the chamber ready to deliver the address. He looked at me in the public gallery where I sat as if to assure me that he was not going to disappoint.

He began his presentation.

His voice projection was good, so was his body language and body movements.

"I, as President of this Republic, want to leave a legacy. I, therefore, commit to work very hard to tirelessly build that legacy especially that my current tenure is only three years," he said amidst cheers of approval from MPs.

"I will not hesitate to part ways with those not prepared to pull their weight in the crusade to move our country forward," he warned.

I remember I insisted that he should include that line because some senior government officials still considered him a rank outsider despite being President. They were bent on undermining him.

As delivery gained momentum, the President accidentally flipped the pages off the podium and they flew onto the floor. The orderly delivery was disturbed as was the order of the pages.

Opposition lawmakers booed as his Aide-De-Camp moved to pick up the 75 pages from the floor.

"Order!" the Speaker shouted to calm the noisy parliamentarians.

I quickly dashed to the chamber with the spare copy of the speech that I had carried, passed it on to the ADC who placed it on the podium. Some of the pages on the floor were left uncollected.

After that short interruption, the President resumed delivery.

"Mr. Speaker…" the lawmakers from the governing party cheered.

The incident was a big lesson for me.

I then made it mandatory to carry a spare copy of the speech at every event where the President would speak just in case something similar happened.

After parliament adjourned, the President invited me for lunch at his home

"That was incredible!" he said as he shook my hand.

I had saved him embarrassment.

Subsequently, I bound all such speeches into a booklet to avoid a similar occurrence.

******

The following day I was back in the office and sent out a circular to all government departments demanding that any draft speech for the President should reach my office at least two weeks before the event. If it was delivered late, I would not allow the President to officiate.

I also ordered that draft speeches be not more than 20-pages.

The President supported my proposal.

But implementation proved difficult with the exception of three or four ministries. Speeches continued to land on my desk late in total disregard of my instructions.

The President was on me.

"I will not allow you to bring a speech to me a night before the event. You have to be tough with these people," he said.

Often, the Chief of Staff would remind me that my position was higher than the Permanent Secretaries so that I could supervise or instruct them to perform to my satisfaction.

"Use your powers young man," Dr. Austin Sichinga would say when he heard me complain about delayed speeches.

I noticed that it was a trend to send documents to State House late.

Some heads of state are comfortable with reading a speech which they have had no occasion to go through.

But President Banda was not.

"I will never read a speech which I have not seen in advance," the President insisted.

Twice, we had to cancel events because Cabinet Office delivered the speeches late. Those cancellations, to some degree, helped drive change of the work culture in the public service as far as presidential involvement was concerned.

Another problem was the tradition of Cabinet Ministers to speak before the President at public events. The aim was to introduce the topic and call upon the head of state to deliver the keynote address.

However, ministers had the tendency to pre-empt the President by announcing all key issues, leaving the President to merely regurgitate the same.

I observed it at a number of events. I became concerned that impact of the President's message was being diluted.

My job was to make the President look good!

I raised the matter with him and without debate, he agreed with me.

"You have to raise it in Cabinet," he said.

Cabinet meetings were held on Mondays and by virtue of my position, I attended cabinet meetings and contributed through the President.

At the following Cabinet meeting, the President raised the issue. He asked me to address the Cabinet on the matter. All unanimously supported my suggestion.

It was always like that if the President supported an issue. Very few ministers would disagree and sometimes the President spoke last in order to allow for debate.

The last problem we had to deal with in connection with speeches was the local leadership of the governing party. Whenever the President toured the countryside, party leaders used the event to inform the President of local problems which tended to embarrass the head of state.

"Mr. President, here we have no water. People have no jobs here. Government has failed to help them," a party official would say, with huge applause from the crowd.

After such remarks the President was forced to abandon his written speech and address the concerns raised. Most of the times, the President had no prior knowledge of those problems and therefore no immediate solutions.

But President Banda was adaptable. I would quickly consult government officials in order to answer the issues raised and within a short time, the President would speak fluently to the issues.

This became a subject for later discussion with the President.

"We need political education in our party," the President said.

"The local leadership should be telling people what government is doing to help resolve problems. Not to stir up trouble through such speeches."

We had to develop a working relationship with party leaders so that they would raise issues well in advance prior to planned visits.

That enabled us to draft the President's speeches with specific local issues, problems and suggested solutions in mind.

CHAPTER FIVE
THE WORKS OF MY HAND

A group of tourists gathered at the entrance to the Royal Livingstone Hotel in the city of Livingstone, Southern Zambia when word went round that the President would be coming for a brief meeting. With their cameras and smartphones, they positioned themselves to take the best shots of the President as he arrived.

"Can we take a photograph with the President?" they asked the presidential guards who just shoved them away.

As the motorcade approached, the tourists burst into cheers and attempted to move closer to the President but the security prevented them.

"Please leave them, they are our visitors," the President said as he alighted from his vehicle. He waved to them to come closer.

He posed for photographs with them. Those who had remained in the restaurant also rushed out for the photo opportunity with the President. Afterwards the President joined them for a meal in the restaurant.

"Why did you choose Zambia?" he asked an elderly couple from the United States.

"Zambia is beautiful and we heard a lot about the Victoria Falls," one of them answered.

The Victoria Falls is one of the seven natural wonders of the world, located on the border between Zambia and Zimbabwe.

The tourists used the rare opportunity with the President to discuss the difficulties they encountered in obtaining Zambian visas. They said the process was cumbersome.

"Dickson, come and sit with me here," he called out to me from among the aides who sat a few tables away.

"It's difficult to get a visa into Zambia," a tourist said.

They told the President that it sometimes took weeks for Zambian embassies to process visa applications and this discouraged tourists from considering Zambia as the destination of choice despite what the country had to offer.

"We need to make immediate changes to visas," the President said as he listened attentively.

When we returned to Lusaka, he requested a cost-benefit analysis of the visa fees from the Minister of Finance. The report showed that visa fees were minimal but affected the tourist inflow because of the cumbersome issuance process. Tourists and investors from the Middle East for instance had to apply for their visas at the Zambian mission in Egypt and it took several weeks.

"I have abolished the visa fees," he remarked after reading the report.

He said they were a hindrance to the growth of tourism.

"All visas should be issued at the point of entry," he ordered.

******

Two months after those decisions were made they were still not implemented and the President was not happy about it. He asked me to convene a meeting of the departments of Treasury and Immigration as well as other security agencies and the Ministry of Tourism.

He wanted to know why his instructions were not being followed.

"We use the visa system to scan for possible terrorists and for people on the international wanted list," one security official said.

He was supported by officials from the Ministry of Foreign Affairs who said visa fees were also used to run embassies when there were delays in bank transfers.

The President was not convinced and stood his ground.

"I have made the decision and it is final," he said.

The Minister of Finance Dr. Situmbeko Musokotwane supported the President as the impact on the Treasury would be minimal. The working basis for the decision was that increased tourist arrivals would benefit the country more than increased collections from visa fees.

"Dickson explain to them what we saw in Emirates," the President said.

He was referring to a visit we undertook to Ras al-Khaimah, one of the smaller components of the United Arab Emirates where we found that tourism was fast approaching a boom.

"We just removed the visa fees and everyone is flocking here," the crown prince and deputy ruler Sheikh Saud Bin Saqr al Qasim had told us.

Inside the Presidency

The only requirement was that tourists spent not less than US$1,000 dollars per visit.

The area is essentially a desert and has only artificial game parks yet it attracts a huge number of tourists, far more than Zambia which has natural vegetation and a wide array of animal species.

******

After the visa issue was settled the President decided to make a number of changes to the government system to make it more responsive. He said he was in a hurry to develop the country especially because he had only three years in office.

"I want to make a difference," he said.

His next area of interest was the short budget cycle.

The budget was presented to the National Assembly in February and funds released in April of each year and cycle then ran until December.

Almost invariably government departments failed to utilize the allocations due to the short cycle.

"Why is it like that?' he asked.

It has always been so since 1964 when Zambia became independent and it was enshrined in the constitution, he was told. He was not persuaded.

"I am convinced that a change will improve budget management since implementation of programmes will then begin in January allowing a full year for implementation," he argued.

He instructed Members of Parliament to amend the constitution according to his suggestion. An amendment was duly table and went through smoothly with even opposition lawmakers supporting the change.

That goal achieved, he turned his attention to infrastructure development. His first initiative was to provide health care close to the people especially in the rural communities. Using a loan from the Indian government, the President rolled out the construction of health posts in areas with a population of at least 500 to 3000 across the country.

"The distribution of health and other facilities in this country is still skewed towards urban areas," he said when announcing the plan.

He also ordered mobile hospitals as an interim measure while the construction of health posts was underway.

"*Nchito za manja yanga* (the work of my hands)" the President often said in reference to the multiple projects that he launched in his three-years in office.

But while he was rolling out the projects, the country was hit by a crippling fuel shortage in October 2009 that threatened the economy. The country's sole refinery, which at the time produced 24,000 barrels per day, broke down. Imports of finished products were not encouraged to protect the refinery and were not too profitable because of the high taxes levied on them.

Long vehicle queues formed at service stations around the country. The shortage was so serious that some motorists spent nights at petrol stations in order to be sure of supply if fuel was delivered. But there were no deliveries for days.

Unemployed youths cashed in and bought whatever they could for resale at a premium. That business boomed as stranded motorists fought over the little fuel that was available on the black market.

Heavy industries, including copper mines, recorded declines in output as a result of the crisis.

"The President is incompetent," the opposition leader Michael Sata said.

Sata even joined the cheering motorists on a long queue in Lusaka while he attacked the government for poor handling of the crisis. His pictures were splashed in newspapers. He was shown carrying a jerry can while another opposition leader resorted to cycling to highlight the crisis.

It was one of the biggest crises for the new President.

He held several meetings with the cabinet and experts in energy to try and end the shortage as demands for his resignation increased.

"The import duty on fuel has been suspended for two weeks to allow oil marketing companies to bring in fuel at a lower price," the President announced as he sought to ease the shortage.

The shortages ended eventually but the President used the crisis to revamp the entire fuel supply chain.

"I don't want to experience any such shortages in my presidency again," he told his Ministers.

He immediately embarked on the construction of fuel storage facilities across the country to hold strategic reserves for at least 30 days in case of shortages.

"Why is the cost of Coca-Cola uniform across the country while fuel is not?" the President asked the rather rhetorical question.

Various explanations were given but he was again not convinced. "I want fuel to cost the same across the country," he said.

Within weeks, a system for uniform pricing was worked out and was immediately implemented. Pump prices for fuel became uniform countrywide at his instigation.

He also tasked his Energy Minister Kenneth Konga to look for cheaper sources of crude oil including the possibility of importing from neighbouring Angola, Nigeria and Venezuela.

******

The opening of new mines led to increased demand for electricity. Domestic consumption surged as well. In the three years of his tenure for instance he commissioned production at the Lumwana Copper Mine, a huge open cast mine in northwestern Zambia. Another huge copper mine, Kalumbila was under construction in the same area.

He further spearheaded the development of the Multi Facility Economic Zones (MFEZ), diversified, tax free industrial parks. Many times the MFEZs entailed the creation of new companies for both domestic and export-oriented industries that required adequate supply of electricity to sustain growth.

The state-run power monopoly, the Zambia Electricity Supply Corporation (ZESCO) began rationing supply in the ultimately infamous 'load shedding' programme which was about rolling power blackouts.

It was clear that investment in new power generation and expansion of existing plants was needed urgently. The President now focused on power projects preferably under private-public partnerships. The result of this push was the beginning of the construction of the 120MW Itezhi-tezhi power station, a joint venture of ZESCO Ltd and Tata Africa. Other power projects were the expansion of Kalungiwshi, Lusiwasi and Lunzua power stations. New power stations were sited at Kabompo Gorge in the northwest and the massive 750MW Kafue Lower power station outside Lusaka was to be built jointly with the Chinese.

The President also arranged for free solar panels, which were distributed to various households in order to help reduce demand for electric power.

******

"Hungry people are angry people," the President would often say when talking about food production in the country. Himself a farmer, the President prioritized agriculture, especially support for small-scale farmers. This was mainly done as subsidies in the form of fertilizer and seed under the Farmer Input Support Programme (FISP). This did not go down well with the International Monetary Fund (IMF) and the World Bank. The duo's position was that subsidies were retrogressive and distorted the national budget.

Despite their displeasure, the President would not budge.

"Provision of inputs to small scale farmers through the FISP is critical to Zambia's food security," he argued.

The programme was generally a success and contributed to food security. The result was that small-scale farmers produced more maize than the government budgeted for purchase through the Food Reserve Agency (FRA).

"Minister, let us buy all the maize from our people," the President would often say to the Minister of Finance.

Under his stewardship a number of food storage facilities were rehabilitated and new ones were built for the strategic food stocks. These were essential to fall back on in times of drought.

With enough grain in the country, a school-feeding programme was developed under his tutelage and school-going children in rural areas got government-paid meals at school.

The programme, which has been successful in Brazil, was meant to improve school attendance. Its success underlines its popularity to date in most parts of the country.

******

The President pushed for the construction of new schools in each and every district of the country. He also advocated for skills development colleges for high school leavers. Several new schools were constructed and over 5,000 teachers were recruited within the three-years of his tenure. A focus on the development of training programmes for the physically challenged was also developed. Construction started of two boarding schools in Lusaka for that purpose.

******

"Mr. President, how can we participate in all these developments taking place at home?" a Zambian living in Canada asked. "Almost all successive Zambian governments never involved the diaspora in national programmes, he added.

"We want to be part of the programme," one person from the diaspora said when the President met a group of Zambians living in Canada.

After their short presentation, the President was moved and determined that Zambians living abroad should have the opportunity to participate in national development. He agreed to support the clause in the constitution for dual-citizenship which is currently prohibited in Zambia.

"We need every Zambian to be part of the development process regardless of where they are," the President later said when he invited for lunch a group of Zambians living abroad.

As a first step, he offered them land as an incentive for them to invest back in the country.

He also created an office within State House to coordinate matters of Zambians in the diaspora such as efficient passport renewals, land application and harnessing project ideas from them.

"From the many meetings I have had with Zambians abroad, I am convinced that our people wherever they may be are proud Zambians and we should embrace them as they wish to participate in the building of our economy," the President said.

He appointed Ms. Ngoza Munthali, an economist, to head a diaspora office at State House.

******

The President's push to transform the country within his three year term began to bear fruits. Jobs were created in the construction industry as more schools, hospitals, shopping malls and roads were earmarked for construction. The government now faced budgetary pressures for extra funding to maintain the momentum.

Dubbed 'Formula One', the roads project he launched was aimed at tarring all urban roads while opening up the country with new major highways.

But the cost exceeded the resources at hand.

"We need to get additional funding for the roads and other infrastructure," he said.

The plan called for an investment of US$1.6 billion over ten years to cover 40,000 kilometres of road across the country.

The Finance Minister Dr. Musokotwane suggested borrowing on the international money market, a proposal that was endorsed by cabinet.

Arrangements began for the first-ever Eurobond for Zambia but it was only floated months after the President left office. The bond raised US$750 million and was oversubscribed more than 15 times.

The President insisted for the sovereign credit rating for the country ahead of the Eurobond. Two respectable rating agencies, Standard and Poor's and FITCH gave the country's economy and political environment a B plus rate, which helped in the floatation of the bond.

Eyebrows were raised over the multi-billion dollar projects that the President undertook and there were questions about the source of funds.

"Government will have to borrow beyond the budgetary ceilings which will certainly worsen the country's debt burden," said Sydney Mwansa of the Catholic Jesuit Centre for Theological Reflections (JCTR), which monitored foreign debt management.

******

With increased projects, the demand for land also increased.

The President directed the opening up of new areas for development, especially the establishment of commercial farming blocks.

"I want Zambia to be the biggest exporter of beef to Europe. We have plenty of land and water," he said when announcing the launch of the Nansanga Farming bloc in Central Zambia.

He invited international companies to bid for farms in the block where they would set up ranches as well as produce a wide array of crops. Zambians would be provided with capital to set up support services to the new farms.

The President even established a specific ministry to deal with livestock development and disease control.

In Luapula Province in the north of the country, a biogas and biofuel project was to be undertaken by the Brazilians, who were interested in setting up sugarcane and jatropha plantations.

To further reinforce these efforts, the President encouraged tax holidays to deserving companies using the existing incentives of the Zambia Development Agency (ZDA).

For instance, Pepsi Cola reopened a manufacturing plant in Zambia after many years of absence. The project was granted a five-year tax concession by the government when it opened the US$44 million factory.

The focus was to make Zambia a regional hub for industrial development. In 2011 the President launched the construction of the multi-million Hitachi plant in Lusaka, a Japanese manufacturing company, which has since opened. The company re-manufactures large-scale mining equipment for exports within the Southern Africa region.

There was more.

A new airport was planned with a Turkish company. The task was to undertake a project that would turn Lusaka into an international transit and transfer centre for different airlines. At the same time the Chinese aircraft manufacturing company, CATIC International, would open a service centre in Zambia.

"I hope Zambians will give us the chance to complete these projects," the President would occasionally say after the launch.

CHAPTER SIX

DEALING WITH SCANDALS

Viewed from within government, they didn't look like scandals but to the trouble makers in the opposition. But when they took on the aura of scandal, we in government, nonetheless, took them seriously. They tainted the image of the President.

During President Banda's 3-year tenure, there were three events that acquired notoriety as "scandals". They kept us occupied for their duration.

There were allegations of impropriety by a member of the president's family in an alleged US$100 million arms deal and there were the "struggles" around the privatization of the state-owned telecommunications company, ZAMTEL.

The alleged embezzlement of US$2million, mainly aid money, at the Ministry of Health was another scandal that gripped the nation. Some donors withheld support to the health sector and the matter came to be considered as one of the biggest financial scandals in the public service. Some suggested that it was only the tip of the iceberg!

On day, I was taking a cold shower shortly before 6.30 hours, when I noticed three missed calls on my mobile phone. – The President was trying to reach me!

Unless there was something urgent, it was unusual for the 'Principal', as we called him, to call directly and early in the morning for that matter.

The missed calls gave me a rush of adrenaline. With urgency, I called him back. Soon he was on the line.

"What are you doing about this story? It is a lie. I have never bought arms," he said in a hoarse voice. He sounded angry.

He must have been coming out of the gym. Early morning gym sessions before breakfast and long hours of office work were a daily routine for the then 74 year-old.

I was caught unawares. I had not read through the morning newspapers that early and had therefore no inkling of what the President was on about. I asked for time and he obliged.

I was immediately upset with the presidential valet for ignoring my clear instructions not to give the President newspapers without my saying so. It was my responsibility to scan the press and provide a brief with suggested responses to major stories. That way, the President would always know that he was in safe hands and that his public relations team was proactive.

I quickly dressed up and en-route to the office bought the newspapers from a kiosk. They were normally delivered to my office but with that early morning call from the 'boss', I would not have waited.

My automatic Mitsubishi Pajero came in handy. In the morning rush hour traffic, I was able to accelerate, one hand on the steering wheel while I scanned stories.

The story in question was carried by the privately owned daily newspaper, *The Post*. Under a screaming headline, it quoted the former Defence Minister George Mpombo who had resigned his post a year earlier as saying that he had quit because President Banda wanted him to sign a US$100 million arms supply contract with a South African firm. He claimed that the president's eldest son, James, was to get a ten percent commission on the contract.

"It was absolutely dirty, a hanky-panky sort of deal," the paper quoted Mpombo as saying.

It was clear that the story was timed to do the maximum damage to the president, coming as it did barely five months from a crucial general election.

The president's anger was thus understandable. He now wanted damage control from his spin-doctor. I was on the spot.

The story seemed credible coming from one who was the number three man in the government hierarchy and who had resigned in what were still unclear circumstances.

While on the road, I telephoned the Defence Minister Dr. Kalombo Mwansa just to be doubly sure that Zambia had not acquired any arms during President Banda's tenure. He too was shocked by the allegation. The story was a total fabrication. At no time did Zambia procure arms during the president's tenure nor was there any intention to do so.

By 09:00 hours, my office inbox was full with press queries from both local and international media while my landline kept buzzing.

It was the main story of the day and the press wanted my comment! One of my assistants, Charles Kachikoti, alerted me of the various radio phone-in programmes that day. All were on the same subject: the arms deal.

"President Banda is a thief," a caller would say just like that.

Private radio stations had mushroomed but most lacked the professional knowhow on handling live phone-ins. Slander was common.

Internet blogs qually had a field day attacking the President and calling for his resignation for wasting over US$100 million on the procurement of arms when the majority of Zambians were living in abject poverty.

Another day of firefighting, I sighed.

It has become almost routine. My days in State House as spokesman and advisor mostly revolved around dealing with negative press reports to the virtual exclusion of everything else. Putting out the fire had become an everyday issue. The work was also taking a toll on my health. For the first time, my blood pressure was detected to be too high!

On this day, before I could get back to the President with a counter strategy, the other "un-appointed advisors" had preceded me. There are plenty of such from the governing party or job seekers eager to enhance their prospects with the administration. They are normally very charming and have a knack of moving smoothly from one president to the next. They also despise official advisors and are impatient with the official process. They tell a President only what he wants to hear!

But President Banda trusted his team and he promptly channeled unsolicited advice to this team.

"Let's just ban the *Post* newspaper," one had advised.

But could that be the answer to negative publicity?

I didn't agree with that reasoning especially since newspaper banning had been tried elsewhere in Africa without success. A good example Zambia's neighbour Zimbabwe which had pushed a hardline on the foreign press, including closing down their offices in Harare. However negative publicity only increased. Personally, I believed in engaging the media although the results were not always immediate.

The law in Zambia allows the President to proscribe a publication. Zambia's second President, the late Frederick Chiluba, once exercised that power and banned one edition of *The Post* but that did not solve much.

The national security services had suggested to President Banda when he was elected in 2008 that they acquire Chinese technology to block critical websites and blogs. However, after a lengthy debate, it was agreed that it was not the way to go in a democracy.

"Just leave them, they will get tired," the President would respond when pressed to deal with the growing negative publicity.

By midday, I was with the President in his tiny semi-oval office. The walls were covered with wooden panels while his personal standard – a huge orange flag with an Eagle – fluttered behind his chair.

"I have drafted a press release to respond to the story," I told the President who sat looking at me quietly. He was always a good listener.

After I was done with my presentation, I discovered that he had had a change of heart.

"I think let's not respond. People will see through these lies," he said calmly. Such was the challenge of working as President Banda's spin-doctor.

Clearly, he had overcome the early morning anger and now treated the story as a bygone.

He always trusted the Zambian people to see through such fabrications on their own.

"No sir, we need to respond," I would insist on occasion and sometimes there was a back and forth between us.

I had earned the reputation of offering an alternative view on some issues, especially governance-related ones. I had the background of having worked with a number of civil society organizations as well as the local and foreign press and tried to put across their views to the President whenever an opportunity arose.

In the end, the President appreciated my input because he had an alternative view from within his circle.

On this day, after a lengthy debate, we resolved that my statement be issued by the Defence Minister. However, the national intelligence and the defense force command were not ready to engage the public on issues of arms procurement – whether the story was true or false.

"We don't discuss our military capability in the press," one army General responded to my proposed statement.

As mentioned earlier in 1999, I was among a dozen journalists arrested and charged with espionage over a story that detailed Zambia's military capability compared to neighbouring Angola.

And here I was again trying to convince the same military that the image of the Commander in-Chief and President of the Republic of Zambia was at stake unless something was said.

We needed to defend the President.

"This story will not just die on its own. We need to explain ourselves to the nation," I pushed my position at a meeting convened to discuss the issue.

The military believed in too much secrecy and hardly gave media statements even when they needed to. Many countries in Africa have opened up on this front. The South African defense force, for example, gives routine media updates on various issues concerning their operations.

After a back and forth discussion and telephone consultations, I managed to win the hearts of the Generals. It came a shaded too late. By the end of the day, the canard had become the 'truth' as a result of the delay in responding. Our statement did little to change public perceptions because we responded late.

"Why has the President failed to respond himself?" Given Lubinda, an opposition lawmaker, asked.

Again it was alleged that the failure by the President to respond was because he was involved in the deal through his son.

The opposition perpetuated that line and it became a pre-campaign issue as the 2011 general elections approached.

"Rupiah Banda is corrupt," insisted his main challenger, the leader of the Patriotic Front party Michael Sata throughout the campaign. He eventually won the polls to become Zambia's fifth President.

Banda's son, James, sued Mpombo for defamation of character in the Lusaka High Court over the story. The court only ruled in his favour a year after his father had left office.

Irreversible damage had been done.

******

After the arms deal debacle, another of supposedly President Banda's scandals emerged.

A key minister and ally of the President had to quit her job following a report that a tribunal has been set up to probe her conduct in office. This was barely three months after being sworn in. The issue was her handling of the initial stages of the privatization of ZAMTEL. The story began with a leakage to the press that Transport and Communications Minister Dora Siliya had signed an agreement with a Cayman Island registered company for the valuation of the assets of the company but that the agreement was signed in breach of procedure. Apparently, the Attorney General had advised the minister not to sign the agreement unless certain issues were addressed. But she was alleged to have ignored that advice.

A former minister, together with a consortium of civic groups, petitioned the Chief Justice to appoint a tribunal under the Parliamentary and Ministerial Code of Conduct Act to investigate the minister's conduct. Among the allegations against the minister was that she had awarded a US$2 million contract to RP Capital without following tender procedures.

The tribunal was appointed on February 25, 2009 led by Supreme Court Judge Dennis Chirwa. During its public sittings, the story took a twist and the President became the subject. His third born son, Henry, was mentioned by one witness as being connected to the Cayman Island-based company. The implication was clear. Henry must have introduced them to the Minister and possibly influenced her to sign the deal.

At the end of the sittings, the tribunal cleared the minister on a number of allegations. However, it found that the minister had in fact committed the serious offence of breaching the constitution when she ignored the Attorney-General's advice. This conclusion by the tribunal appeared to go beyond its mandate. The investigation had specific terms of reference. These did not include determining whether or not the minister had breached the constitution.

"With regard to the general law, we have already said that in the first place, Siliya should not have been involved in the selection of RP Capital and valuation of ZAMTEL assets," the report read.

Instead of finalizing the matter, the tribunal left the final decision to the president.

"In the present case, we leave Hon. Siliya's breaches to His Excellency the President to deal with," the report read.

The proposed sale of ZAMTEL became a hot political potato.

The company was one of the few remaining state enterprises and it was the case that most of those that had been sold rapidly shut down. So, Zambians were wary of privatization given the trend.

The allegations of corruption in the sale generated a media frenzy. It had a field day!

"Why is the President not firing the Minister?" a press query was raised.

"Is the President protecting the Minister because his son is implicated in the deal?" asked the next one to pop up.

We had to go into overdrive to fight the sustained battle that followed.

Firstly, the Minister had to give way in order for us to safeguard the President's image. His apparent reluctance to fire her, as seen by others, was equivalent to condoning corruption.

April 21, 2009 was for me a sad day as I was the one tasked to handle the issue. The Minister was close to both the President and me.

We knew each other since our days as practicing journalists before she joined politics. She was also the spokesperson of the governing party and so we naturally consulted each other often on media approaches.

Before this, the President had openly defended her at a media briefing, which led the opposition to conclude that she was in the deal with the 'boss'.

"*Rupiah, his sons and Dora are guilty over Zamtel sale*" read the *Post* headline of June 16, 2010.

Some ministers also thought the President was too lenient with her.

"You deal with this matter," the President said to me.

The instruction came after we had our own internal meeting where it was unanimously agreed that the President should respect the tribunal findings even though the judges went beyond their powers.

We leave the breaches of the minister to the President to deal with!

"Breach of the constitution and the laws made thereunder by ministers and officials undermines the rule of law and contaminates the government system," the tribunal had said.

So we had to deal with the issue in a pragmatic manner.

A meeting was called at State House, which I chaired. The President did not attend. The legal advisor to the President was called in as a backup as we met the Minister and her lawyers. The meeting was lengthy but after persuasion, she agreed to quit. We also agreed that she should challenge the decision of the tribunal in the High Court because it had gone beyond its mandate.

The President didn't want to sack her because he believed she had not done anything wrong. He had also defended her action on record.

She was the victim of politics and I shared that view.

After the meeting, I quickly consulted the President and released a news statement.

"The President wishes to announce to the nation that he has received a letter of resignation from Honorable Siliya, who has decided to step down in view of the tribunal's findings," part of the statement read.

But her departure only heightened the pressure on the President.

"The President must resign too!" a consortium of NGOs led by Transparency International demanded.

The opposition went through the motions of organizing numbers in parliament to bring an impeachment motion against the President whom they accused of being part of the telecom deal through his son. The impeachment attempt flopped.

But pressure still mounted.

We worked on different media strategies to deal with the developing situation.

I gave out exclusive interviews to carefully selected reporters, issued press statements as well as leaflets to explain the matter.

The story was really consuming us.

The workers threatened to strike indefinitely following allegations of corruption and the perception that the President had an interest in the matter.

The decision to sell the company was based on strong grounds. It was on the verge of collapse due to debts and overemployment.

"President Banda appealed to the nation not to lose sight of the various and difficult problems affecting ZAMTEL and in particular the workers' plight," I said in my April 21, 2009 statement.

"The President observed that the state-owned company has continued to incur huge debts which needed to be liquidated or the situation would get out of hand."

At that time, the company had liabilities in excess of US$100 million, 2,505 employees – three times higher than private operators.

It had 272,000 subscribers for both mobile and fixed lines while private firms had ten times that number.

The government needed to pump in US$200 million to recapitalize the company if it had to survive. So, privatization seemed the only reasonable route to go.

But all these considerations were ignored in the imbroglio. Emphasis came to be on the Minister's action to sign the agreement against the advice of the Attorney General and Cabinet in violation of the Zambian constitution and cabinet regulations.

On June 18, 2009, the High Court set aside the findings of the tribunal after she argued successfully that the tribunal recommendations were beyond the legal mandate of the tribunal. Following this outcome, the President re-appointed her to the cabinet as Education Minister, prompting more attacks from the anti-graft watchdog. On our part we made the case that she had been cleared by the courts!

The President quite boldly decided to table the ZAMTEL issue before Cabinet for approval to proceed with privatization. It was decided that government should sell 75 percent shares to a private equity partner who would be picked through a competitive bid. The remaining 25 percent shares were to be floated on the Lusaka Stock Exchange.

It was a solid plan. However, in retrospect, I believe we should have suspended the process, even if temporarily, in view of the allegations. The bad publicity never went away.

After cabinet approval the President decided to face the dispirited workers.

It was June 24, 2009.

We sat in the small and poorly ventilated canteen at the company's head office in Zambia's second city, Ndola, some 400 kilometers from Lusaka. Over one hundred workers attended, some followed the proceedings from the windows. The atmosphere was tense.

Police officers, in full riot gear, were stationed nearby in case the situation turned ugly. You could tell from the workers's faces that they were despondent. The national anthem was sung in muted tones.

The President took to the podium. He had all the statistics with him.

"If the company is allowed to fail, there would be a significant cost of at least US$112 million in direct costs to the tax-payer and loss of employment without terminal benefits," the President told the workers.

Question time:

"Is it true Mr. President that you want to sell the company to your friends?" one visibly angry worker asked.

Calmly, the President took the worker on.

"The selection of a strategic equity partner will be conducted in accordance with the law," the President answered, citing the relevant statutes that governed privatization of state enterprises in Zambia.

On June 5, 2010, the Zambian government announced the sale of the 75 percent stake in ZAMTEL to the Libyan company – LAP Green Networks - at a price of US$257 million. Almost all the workers that were retrenched as a result of the sale were paid their full benefits. It looked like a good deal.

But as fate would have it, the following year, a civil war broke out in Libya that led to the UN Security Council passing a resolution imposing sanctions on Libya. This impacted the project as LAP Green Networks was owned by the Libyan government. It meant funds meant for ZAMTEL were affected.

This was followed by another round of firefighting.

The President set up a committee headed by the Attorney General to look at the legal implications of the UN sanctions and the ZAMTEL agreement. A team was dispatched to New York to discuss with the UN how to save the company.

The issue of the ZAMTEL sale remained hot until the 2011 General elections. When Sata was elected president, one of his first decisions was to reverse the sale on the dubious grounds that the company was sold fraudulently to benefit President Banda and his family.

*****

Just when the President was trying to reorganize the ministry of health to make it more responsive, a corruption scandal came to light. It was a huge scandal that attracted a lot of international media coverage. The scandal centred on allegations that about US$2 million dollars in donor aid had been embezzled at the ministry.

Donors reacted sharply to the alleged theft and immediately suspended over US$300 million funding to Zambia's health sector, money meant largely for HIV/AIDS programmes.

It was of course the President and his government who were ultimately accountable.

"This is ridiculous, I am only three months as President," the President told a meeting of donors who wanted to know his stance on the matter.

The media had created the impression that the money was stolen in the short period since President Banda became President.

Donor aid accounted for more than 50 percent of Zambia's health budget at that time.

"None of the leaders are involved in the theft," President Banda told the donors, and indeed after investigations, fingers pointed at junior and middle-ranking civil servants.

The President ordered their suspension and prosecution but that did not stop his critics from going into overdrive. They attacked him saying he was soft on corruption and that was why junior officers could pocket monies without fear.

He also ordered the treasury to find money and refund the donors the equivalent of the stolen funds. It was one of the conditions for resumption of aid.

CHAPTER SEVEN
MONKEY URINATES ON THE PRESIDENT

For a while President Banda was not seen in public.

The situation in the country was worrying. Medical doctors and nurses were on an indefinite work stoppage to press for better pay and conditions of service.

Civil servants planned similar action.

The price of copper, Zambia's main export and foreign exchange earner was fluctuating downwards, threatening a potentially debilitating economic slowdown.

There was need for the President to address these issues.

My initial plan when I took up the position was to have the President meet the press quarterly, take questions and respond to concerns. But that was not to be. His diary was just too full to accommodate that. Thus, sometimes the President went for months without a news conference.

This time around, I pushed for it. There were too many press queries and the nation wanted him to respond to the gathering crisis, especially as the strike had crippled the health system. One private television station repeatedly showed dead bodies on its main news to illustrate the impact of the strike.

The President had opted to engage labour union leaders quietly and explain the predicament the country faced. But that strategy did not work as the workers accused their leaders of selling out to the President.

"We want to hear the president, not Dickson Jere," one opposition leader said in reference to the numerous interviews and press releases I gave.

Finally, the President agreed that he needed to face the nation.

The press conference was set for 10:00 hours on June 24, 2009.

It was packed.

Members of the press, diplomats, senior government officials and members of the governing party were in attendance. The conference was held on the lawn of State House just outside the president's office. Traditionally, that was the area where they were held.

The gardens were beautiful and the huge trees provided an umbrella shade. The morning sunrays were just heating up when the President began his address.

He was prepared for the event and he spoke confidently while occasionally looking up the trees where a group of monkeys was playing on the branches. They were part of the different species of wild animals and birds kept at State House.

Suddenly, something quite strange and unusual happened! A monkey, which seemed to pick him out as the "main man", urinated on the president! The monkey was up the huge *Mopani* tree in whose shade the President and his staff sat.

"*Ah, kanitundila!* (Ah, it has urinated on me!), the President said while looking up the tree where the monkey stayed put.

"I will give this monkey for lunch to Mr. Sata," he said in jest. "Perhaps these are blessings," he added amidst laughter.

The media made the most of the monkey incident and it became the most important issue from the press conference to the virtual exclusion of the more serious issues that he discussed.

Even the international media hyped the monkey story and almost forgot to report what the President said about the state of the nation.

The clip of the monkey urinating on the President even went viral on the YouTube!

"You mean that's all the press can write from that press conference? Even the *BBC*..." an amused President Banda asked the following day as he browsed through the stories.

The British Broadcasting Corporation (BBC) had a banner headline:

"*Zambia leader hit by 'press leak'*. The introduction to the story was that "a cheeky monkey decided to spend a penny on Zambian President Rupiah Banda – as he held a news conference on the economy in the capital Lusaka."

The Telegraph simply said: "*Monkey urinates on Zambian President.*"

Sky news: "*Cheeky Monkey Urinates on Zambian President*".

The international newswires, Reuters, AFP and AP all had the same line with similar headings.

The president's concerns about the treatment of his press conference were not without a basis. We had spent three days preparing for the event. The President had hoped to use the event to calm down the striking workers and explain his plans to them.

But there we were: the monkey stole the show!

Over time, some Zambian musicians even compiled songs based on the incident of the monkey and the president.

I had to devise a new strategy to bring out the main points of the President's speech. I asked the state-run Zambia National Broadcasting Corporation (ZNBC) to rebroadcast the conference at primetime but edit out the monkey business. Full-page advertisements of the speech were placed in some leading daily newspapers and some summary notes and news releases circulated to various radio stations. I wanted the president's speech to have needed impact but the monkey seemed to have stolen the show and won the attention of the press.

******

Three months after that incident, the monkey and the President were back in the media.

In a yearly routine, the population of monkeys at State House used to be "culled." The process was intended on taming the monkeys' growing numbers, where some were removed to the botanical gardens. When the operation was conducted that year, it was a big story – the President was revenging by evicting the monkeys!

"*Zambia's peeing monkeys evicted,*" was the headline on a BBC story.

The Telegraph headline was: "*Zambian President evicts monkeys from residence after urinating incident.*"

This amused the president.

He was not even aware that monkeys were being relocated from State House.

******

At long last, we agreed to make the President be more easily accessible to the press and public. I pushed for that change although some of my colleagues did not share my view. But I thought the President was confining himself too much to State House. He needed to be seen in action. He needed to interact with the people.

He too, agreed.

I worked out a programme where he would be interviewed by small radio stations across the country. He was the first head of State to be on those programmes. Community radio stations had mushroomed in Zambia and almost every province had one. Western aid donors provided seed capital for some of them as part of development assistance. It was easy for me to make contact with the stations. Most of them worked with me when I was President of the Media Institute of Southern Africa.

The programme with the stations was a success.

The strategy helped the President to see first-hand the problems that journalists in rural communities faced.

Studios were makeshift.

Old chicken egg trays were the soundproofing. Old fans worked as coolers for the analogue equipment that was donated by some European charity.

The staff worked as volunteers with no stipend. Most of them were local teachers or nurses who were chosen to run these community radio stations.

But they were the ready source of information to their communities. Newspapers and television signals did not reach those areas.

The President and I used to squeeze ourselves in those tiny studios for hours.

My role was to drop notes for the 'boss' for answers to various questions that came from the community via the telephone.

The shows were superb. I loved them. After the shows, I used to pay the station for the airtime used. The President also tasked me to fundraise for the stations. The process yielded some laptop computers for some stations.

Outside the station, scores of local people would gather to catch a glimpse of the president.

After the interviews, President Banda mingled with the community, shook hands with some and posed for pictures with others. The security people would panic.

I also organized some exclusive interviews with the foreign press. Some flew in for these interviews while others were arranged in the various countries we visited. We started receiving good feedback from those media engagements.

But somehow we relaxed again.

The president's diary still confined him too much to his office and indoor meetings in State House and that continued to be a source of concern for me. I tried to arrange for some more media access but had to compete with other colleagues who equally had important tasks with the president.

Thus, the President was once again out of the public limelight.

There were issues that needed to be explained. Government had acquired mobile hospitals from China, an acquisition opposed by some people on the grounds that it was wasteful expenditure. The President also came under attack for his perceived softly-softly approach to corruption. I wanted him to speak to these issues.

I talked with him. He agreed to spare an hour to do a one-on-one interview with veteran freelance broadcaster Frank Mutubila. He had done similar ones with the President during the campaign period. I got the questions in advance and discussed them with the president. He had all the answers and was ready for the pre-recorded interview the following day. It was to take place in the 'interview room' at State House.

Everything was set for the 10:00 hours recording.

The room was appropriately rearranged.

It was studio-like with a State House backdrop: Two chairs for the interviewer and the President with lovely flower arrangements on the table. The orange presidential flag and the national one were placed behind the president's chair - a symbol of his authority.

I passed through to check on the arrangements just to be sure. My assistants worked with the crew to set up. I was happy with their work and immediately dashed to Nkhwazi, the official residence of the president.

I used to physically check on him at times when there was a recording to be done.

He had to be in the right attire.

Dark suits and navy-blue shirts were good for the television cameras, I occasionally insisted. The president, in his usual humor, used to respond by saying that he started wearing suits long before I was born.

"Those are out of fashion sir," I, at times, responded.

When I arrived at the residence, I found the President in pyjamas. He had a pile of files and papers on the dining table. He had just finished taking his breakfast.

"We are ready for the recording sir," I said.

He looked surprised.

"Your colleagues didn't tell you?" he asked.

The interview was cancelled last night. My 'colleagues' whom he did not name had convinced him not to appear on the programme unless he had something major to announce. I could not believe what I had just heard!

Why would someone talk to the President about my work without asking me?

I was upset.

"I am sorry, I should have told you myself," the President said.

He could sense my frustration and anger at the turn of events.

"Tell Frank, we will organize another one soon," he said reassuringly.

That day, I went home and never appeared at the office again for the day. I needed to cool down.

Without well-organized news conferences or radio and television interviews the only other media access to the President was through spot interviews at the airport. The President stopped occasionally to speak with the press for a few minutes before he boarded his presidential plane.

I was totally against those spot-interviews and the President knew my position.

Firstly, those interviews were spontaneous and unfocussed. It was difficult to manage or prepare the President for them.

Secondly, the press habitually asked questions that riled the president. When I worked as a reporter, we used to agree to ask the President sticky questions at the airport so that he had no escape. That was my reason for opposing them.

I had agreed with the security to allow only photojournalists to cover the President as he boarded the plane. No interviews.

But I failed on that front. The President himself breached my gag order. He stopped for spot interviews and later saying he felt sorry for the reporters who had camped at the airport for hours, at times in the scorching heat.

"*Nanvwa chifundo* (I felt sorry for them)," the President used to tell me after stopping to speak with reporters. "They have been waiting for hours, I thought I should allow a few questions," he would say when we were airborne.

In my view, those interviews used to be a disaster. At times, the President lost his cool and overreacted to some questions. It was fodders for many! The clips were beamed on television portraying the President as temperamental when the opposite was the truth.

On April 1, 2009 for example, *The Post* newspaper had a headline: "*Post reporter annoys Rupiah.*" It happened when the reporter attempted to ask a question outside the topic the President was discussing with reporters at the airport.

"You are fond of that.... I can assure you, you won't go very far in your career. Let's learn to do things in a proper manner and respect each other," the President said.

And the blame for such "blow-ups" was put squarely on my shoulder. I was failing to manage the President with the airport interviews.

"Why do you allow these abrupt interviews?" was the question I was frequently asked.

At times the President himself agreed with me that the press was overstepping their limits by asking him silly questions when he allowed himself to be interviewed. For instance, a reporter asked the President why he had arrived at the airport late when people had been waiting to see him off for hours.

"I think Dickson you are right, they have other agendas," the angry President used to say when we boarded the plane.

******

Another media issue that haunted my office during that period was the arrest of a journalist for distributing 'obscene materials'. This happened during the industrial action by Ministry of Health personnel. When the workers went on an indefinite work stoppage, the health system almost collapsed. A reporter for the daily *Post* newspaper obtained harrowing images of a woman giving birth without any medical assistance.

Those pictures were circulated. Somehow the images found themselves on my desk and that of the president. One of his private secretaries must have put the envelope containing the photos in the president's office without alerting him of the contents.

He was extremely angry when he saw them.

"This is very unethical and *unAfrican*," he said as he threw the pictures away.

They were very disturbing and gruesome. I had never seen their kind before. They showed the baby emerging from the womb feet first.

As a result the President asked me to convene a meeting of the women's movement.

He raised the issue with them. He was particularly unhappy and concerned that such pictures were circulated on the Internet and none of the organizations in attendance had condemned the parading of the poor helpless woman in labour.

The women leaders were in agreement. They condemned the act of circulating the gruesome pictures.

"We have been extremely shocked and disgusted at the pictures you have circulated of a woman in childbirth," read part of the letter to the *Post* from Marian Munyinda, then chairperson of the Non-Governmental Coordinating Council (NGOCC).

"Not only is it a gross violation of the woman's privacy but more so of the sanctity of human life," the letter to the newspaper added.

On June 24, 2009 when addressing a news conference on the economy, the President drifted off the written text and made off-the-cuff remarks regarding the pictures.

He visibly lost his cool again.

He ordered the police to arrest and charge whoever was behind the circulation of the pictures. He said it was 'pornography' and that it demeaned the status of women in Zambia.

I was the master of ceremony and had a tough a time cooling him down.

"Don't stop me!" the President shouted at me as I interjected and tried to cut his off-the-cuff remarks.

"Shame on you, photographer, who took pictures of our mothers naked! I couldn't look at it. When I looked at it, I threw it away," the President said.

It was my first time I saw him lose his temper like that.

But I did not relent. It was my job to keep him focused.

"Thank your Excellency," I chipped in again to try and cut his remarks.

"I hope those responsible for the law of this country will pursue this matter. This is unacceptable. This is not fair for us to be subjected to trash and call it journalism" he said.

Within a short time, the reporter, Chansa Kabwela, was arrested and charged by the police. She argued that she sent the pictures to government officials in order to bring to their attention the pathetic situation in health institutions as a result of the strike.

She was indicted but was later acquitted for lack of evidence against her. She had denied having circulated the gruesome pictures that were all over the Internet.

While locally many, including some of his critics, agreed with the President on the matter, the international community did not support the arrest of the reporter. They demanded the immediate dropping of charges. During that period, I engaged most of the international media watchdog organizations. They had petitioned the President whom they accused of having instigated the arrest through his comments.

******

Soon the nationwide strikes were over. The copper price had stabilized on the international market and things were looking up. The President had taken credit for the way he handled the economic crisis that had hit the country.

Media attention shifted to the fight against corruption. The President was not showing the toughness required to deal with the vice, critics said. During that period, the President would occasionally be seen in the company of Zambia's second President Frederick Chiluba who was facing corruption charges. When Chiluba was acquitted, the media and civil society groups accused the President of having interfered with the court process to ensure that outcome. All these accusations were totally false but a perception was created.

The attacks increased after the President appointed Michael Mabenga, the governing party national chairman, as deputy minister of Lands. Mabenga had lost a parliamentary election petition in 2001 on the grounds of corruption and the Supreme Court had asked the police to prosecute him.

The appointment did not go down well with many Zambians.

While we were still dealing with the matter, another unplanned incident cropped up.

The governing party invited the President to a fund-raising dinner. The President obliged and attended as Guest of Honor. The party requested to auction some of the President's personal items for huge amounts of money. A seat on the President's table was fought over by businessmen who outbid each other.

While at the dinner, the master of ceremonies announced the last auction of the night. It was lunch with the President with whoever won the bid.

"Going, going, gone!" the master of ceremonies hit the hammer.

A prominent businessman had won the bid. We were not told who it was.

The following morning, the press had a story saying that the President had accepted to have lunch with a well-known corruption-convict, businessman Anuj Kumar Rathi.

The High Court had jailed Rathi for high-level corruption involving the procurement of army uniforms. He was only out on bail pending appeal. Having lunch with the President would have sent a bad signal.

"I didn't even know who won the auction," the President told me when he read the stories.

I had to cancel the date and inform the nation of the president's instruction.

"Since it had come to the attention of the President that the winner of the lunch auction was a known convict, it would be morally unacceptable to go ahead and eat with him," I said in a brief statement.

The President also asked the party to return the funds that were donated by Rathi, saying his government abhorred any form of corruption.

I was happy with that decision. It won the President a lot of praise even from his critics who thought he was demonstrating his opposition to corruption.

******

While the good decision was still being applauded, the corruption-tainted former Prime Minister of Thailand Thaskin Shinawatra landed in Zambia. He wanted to meet the president.

Unknown to me and the president, someone within State House had given Shinawatra an appointment. The President was not happy that such a meeting could be arranged without his knowledge.

"Anyway, I will meet him since you have given him the appointment," he said.

I opposed the meeting.

There was too much pressure and talk that the President was dealing with corrupt people.

"Let someone else meet him, Sir," I suggested.

We had a heated debate on the matter. My colleagues backed the President while I stayed my course. I thought it was unfair to put the President in a difficult situation when he did not know about the appointment.

An hour after my position was "voted" down, the President telephoned me. He had decided not to have the meeting based on my strong views.

"I have thought about it," he said.

That was the character of the President. He listened even to minority positions and usually he would go and think about the issue quietly on his own before making the final decision.

******

The President was really in the spotlight as the media seemed to be on a lookout for only negatives on him.

During his annual Christmas holiday, a presidential entitlement, the President loved spending it in the South Luangwa National Park. In 2008 when he left for his holiday, the media published stories and pictures of his family and other relatives departing for the holiday saying he was abusing state resources by inviting the entire clan for the holiday.

It became a heated story. Questions were asked whether the taxpayers should be expected to pay for the president's elderly children and extended family when the majority of Zambians were living in abject poverty.

"I really can't understand these attacks. I have always spent my Christmas with family even before I became president," he complained after he saw the pictures of his family splashed in the newspaper.

"It's petty politics," he said.

I had to explain to the nation that most people who joined in Mfuwe for the family Christmas lunch had in fact chartered their own aircraft and the government was not involved.

The story was mainly sustained by *The Post*, which was critical of the President even before he was elected. The attacks intensified after the President accused the newspaper editor Fred M'membe of having a grudge against him because the President refused to help him over an outstanding loan he needed to pay back the state-run Development Bank of Zambia (DBZ). The newspaper was a shareholder in a defunct private airline, Zambian Airways, which had obtained loans from DBZ and the bank wanted it repaid. But some saw this demand as aimed at killing the newspaper.

"I don't even know this editor although he attacks me every day," the President would say.

******

"*Man Jailed for Insulting RB*" was a story carried by almost all the newspapers in Zambia.

A 35 year old man, Darius Mukuka, was jailed for 18 months with hard labour by a magistrate for having called the President a fool who had failed to govern the country. The remark was made at a bar when a group of people was watching news.

On seeing the story, the President summoned me to his office.

"What is this?" he asked me while pointing at the story in the newspaper.

Insulting the President in Zambia is a criminal offence under Defamation laws.

"This is silly, how can someone be sent to jail for expressing his opinion on me? He has to be taken out immediately," the President said while ordering his legal advisor to issue a warrant of Presidential pardon.

The following day the accused was out of jail and showered praises to the President for the gesture.

I issued a statement to the media, indicating that the President would not tolerate the arrest and jailing of such people who insult him in public although it was an offence.

"If they cannot insult me who else are they going to insult?" he asked while admitting that the law was archaic.

******

The last controversial media incident I dealt with was the closure of a small but influential radio station in western Zambia. A group of secessionists began a campaign to declare the western part of Zambia an independent state to be called the Royal Kingdom of Barotseland. There was a riot over the matter in the provincial capital Mongu. Here, government vehicles were stoned and torched. The police overreacted (in my view) and two protestors were killed.

Radio Lyambai a local FM station was said to have been at the centre of inciting the situation by consistently featuring the secessionists on its programmes. The government closed down the station for inciting civil strife and the police in a raid, which attracted international news coverage, confiscated radio equipment. President Banda's government was accused of stifling press freedom.

This matter, once again, landed on my desk after the Ministry of Information refused to reopen the station. The station had breached the terms and condition of the broadcasting license. So the license was withdrawn!

My colleagues in the private media reminded me of my media freedom activism before I was appointed to State House.

"Do something," some emails said.

I engaged various stakeholders on the issue. The President allowed me to find a solution and reopen the station. This was after I met with International Press Institute director Alison McKenzie who was in Zambia on a fact-finding mission. I assured her that the station would reopen and the equipment returned.

It was to be one of my last assignments - ordering the reopening of the station, a week before Zambia went to the polls.

CHAPTER EIGHT
FOREIGN TRIPS AND DIPLOMACY

When the President, his family and close aides, converged in a small marquee perched on the lawn of State House for prayers, it was an indication that an overseas trip was in the offing. The Zambia army chaplain conducted the prayer sessions and at times it was the Anglican dean of the Cathedral of the Holy Cross.

Singing and dancing were part of afternoon prayer meetings, usually convened a day before the President took a long haul trip. He believed in asking God for "travelling mercies" although he was not a religious zealot.

After Bible readings and a short sermon, the gathering would disperse to prepare for the trip. This time the President was headed for Brazil.

It was the longest trip he was to undertake in his personal jet.

We always chartered or used commercial airlines for long-haul flights because the official jet was good mainly for short and medium haul. It was a 12-seater Bombardier Challenger Jet.

Only his close aides and security traveled with him. I was a permanent fixture in the team.

At 06:00 hours, the engines rolled for what appeared to be the longest journey ever.

It was a 16-hour flight.

The flight plan included a refueling stopover in Luanda, Angola, before crossing the Atlantic to the small town of Recife, in Brazil for another refueling stop before finally landing in Sao Paulo to start the state visit.

The President was the last head of state to be hosted by the outgoing Brazilian President Luiz Inacio Lulu da Silva.

Inside the plane used to be work, laughter, food and sometimes champagne.

Due to the heavy workload, we avoided hard drinks. The President always told us he had no problem with us drinking as long as we had done our work.

On long flights, he read reports and incoming mail.

Sometimes he dictated letters to his secretary or me.

Some decisions were made in mid-air.

When everyone was quiet on their laptops, or books, the President would break the silence with his usual sense of humour. Then laughter replaced silence in the tiny cabin. He was really good at jokes. He even joked about himself!

He also shared his experiences working as a diplomat and minister under Zambia's founding father, President Kenneth Kaunda.

With his constant jokes, the trip was made shorter.

In Brazil, the President managed to convince the Brazilians to build a plant for the manufacture of generic drugs in Zambia. Specifically, he wanted them to manufacture cheap antiretroviral drugs for HIV/AIDS. He also wooed investors such as the giant mining firm, Vale, to invest in the country. Vale now co-owns Konkola North Copper Mines after investing about US$400 million in the project.

He negotiated for a sugarcane and biofuel project that was to be established in the northern part of the country. The Brazilians were interested.

"There is too much water going to waste in the north. Sugarcane can do well in the region," he said.

He tasked his chief of staff to make sure the project was realized.

******

When Banda became President in November 2008, his first foreign policy priority was to strengthen bilateral relations with Zambia's nine neighbouring countries. His approach was of constructive engagement at presidential level informed by his experience as a former diplomat and Minister for Foreign Affairs. To actualize this, he visited all the neighbouring countries before embarking on visits to far-flung places. Now as president, he was Zambia's Chief Diplomat.

"We need to be in good books with all our neighbours," he would insist.

As a landlocked country, dependent on neighbours for access to the sea, President Banda was emphatic that Zambia needed the cooperation and understanding of her neighbours and was not above practicing "shuttle diplomacy" to attain that goal.

Foreign affairs became one of the strongest backbones of the president. He took international assignments to be just as important as local ones. This meant travelling to several capitals in a short time in a packed schedule. We could in one day be in three different countries on three different assignments. I for instance remember taking off with the President in a predawn flight to Congo Brazzaville for that country's 50th anniversary. By the afternoon we were leaving Brazzaville for a Heads of State summit in Windhoek, Namibia. We were in Maputo, Mozambique the following day for a State Visit.

It was a punishing schedule that we maintained with little sleep or rest. Jetlag was a permanent complaint in the team.

It was these kinds of trips that Zambians came to question.

When is our President visiting Zambia? was one question frequently asked by critics who said he was wasting money on these trips. Some argued that the President was spending too much time in the air and not nearly enough on the ground.

But some of the foreign trips were unavoidable.

On June 10, 2009, for example, the President was scheduled to address the World Economic Forum in Cape Town, South Africa as the guest speaker. The trip coincided with a nationwide strike by health workers. Some Zambians wanted him to cancel the trip in view of the strike at home although it was of course planned long before the strike.

He felt he had to fulfill that particular engagement.

While in Cape Town, the situation at home deteriorated as medical services at public hospitals ground to a halt.

"Should we go back?" he asked members of his delegation after he was briefed about that situation.

It was agreed that he should fulfill the engagement which was over three days.

However, he had a problem with his knee.

It worsened while in South Africa and he was required to undergo minor surgery.

"We need to inform the nation," I told him.

My fear was that any leakage to the press of his admission to hospital would create panic. It could also be exaggerated.

"Who doesn't get sick? Do I really need to explain everything?" he asked.

The consensus came to be that it was a personal issue and health issues were confidential and could be disclosed only with the consent of the patient.

My colleagues also felt it should be kept confidential.

I disagreed with them.

I explained to the President the implications if the story leaked.

"I don't think it will be right to be reacting to stories. We need to be proactive and announce that the President was in hospital," I pushed on.

I reminded colleagues that the sickness and eventual death of Banda's predecessor, Levy Mwanawasa, had not been handled properly in my view. It caused panic when he was prematurely pronounced dead by the South African media because there were no official updates.

The nation ought to know, I insisted.

In any case, the president's condition was not life threatening. It was only a knee that had troubled him for some days.

He eventually agreed with me.

I released a brief statement from Cape Town on June 11, 2009.

"Medical Doctors who conducted an orthopaedic procedure called arthroscopy on the president's right knee said the minor operation was very successful. The President is expected to make a complete and full recovery within a short period of time," it read.

In my assessment the news and the two updates I gave were well received. It was rare for the nation to be informed of the president's hospitalization.

But there were also questions about why he would have the operation in South Africa when the same could be performed in Zambia. Others thought it was wrong to "rush" for medical attention in a foreign country during a crippling strike by health workers at home. The president's action was sending wrong signals about Zambian health sector.

From that time on all medical treatment or checkups of the President were all announced well in advance to quash speculation. It was one of the areas I helped demystify - the President's treatment was no longer a State secret.

He was soon discharged but there were more misfortunes on the way.

We boarded a chartered jet and were ready for takeoff when the plane developed a fault.

Although it was around 17:00 hours, it was very dark due to heavy rains.

"I am sorry I can't take the risk. We will arrange for another plane, which will be here in the next two hours," the chief pilot said.

We went into our vehicles and headed back to the hotel to wait. It was total confusion, as we had to re-book our rooms after having checked out.

Four hours later, we were airborne in another aircraft.

It was a memorable trip as the President kept us laughing throughout the bumpy flight. He lay on his seat-cum-flatbed to keep the leg, with stitches, upright.

When we landed in Lusaka, there were no nosy photographers to take a shot of the President being lifted from the plane to the waiting presidential car, as he could not walk on his own as a result of the operation.

I was happy. There was no opportunity for negative pictures

******

The President maintained a busy international schedule.

He was elected chairman of the Southern Africa Development Community (SADC) Organ on Politics, Defense and Security, which was responsible for conflict resolution in the region. He had to travel often to South Africa, Botswana, Mozambique and Namibia for several meetings aimed at bringing lasting peace in the Democratic Republic of Congo, Madagascar and Zimbabwe.

The meetings were usually lengthy.

One meeting on the political situation in Zimbabwe that he chaired in Pretoria, South Africa, started at 10:00 hours and only ended at 07:00 hours the next morning. With such unpredictable schedules, it was difficult to plan the president's diary in advance.

"Peace in Zimbabwe means peace for Zambia. The two countries are Siamese twins," he declared at the end.

It was President Banda who played a major role in convincing Zimbabwe's opposition leader Morgan Tsvangirai to join the government of national unity with President Robert Mugabe.

"Your President is a very humble man," said a hotel manager at Pretoria's Hilton Hotel after he saw the President greeting workers who had come to catch a glimpse of him.

It was characteristic of the President always bid farewell to hotel staff by shaking their hands. On such trips, he ate in the common dining area while other presidents remained in their suites.

"You are lucky to work with such a man," the hotel cleaner said as President Banda left the hotel.

The President was also elected chairman of the International Conference of the Great Lakes Region (ICGLR), another regional peace and security organisation, headquartered in Bujumbura, Burundi.

It meant frequent travels to the region for meetings.

The ICGL assignment involved resolving issues in the DRC, Rwanda, Burundi, Sudan and Congo Brazzaville. It was quite involving and punishing for both the President and his delegation.

"Learn from these experiences about the importance of peace," he would say often on these trips.

A country like Burundi suffered from the ravages of civil strife. Infrastructure was destroyed. Bullet-riddled army trucks at the airport were a reminder of the brutal civil war that the country was recovering from.

The new President Pierre Nkurunziza was youthful and sounded eager to make a difference. He became a friend and we regularly exchanged notes especially on football.

There were no decent hotels to sleep in.

Burundi was strategic for Zambia. Almost all the products ranging from food to construction materials were imported from Zambia via Lake Tanganyika. The President had an interest in stability in Burundi in order to grow that trade.

At the time, there were only four Zambian families living in Bujumbura. As per tradition, the President met with Zambians living in the countries he visited. He had a meal with those who made it to the "Meet the President" dinner.

Such gatherings tended to expose the inefficiency in Zambian missions abroad. Many who met with the President complained of ill treatment by embassy staff and that most missions were not taking consular duties seriously.

"Your first priority is to look after Zambians," the President would counsel the diplomats and jotted down the concerns raised.

Besides his role as peacemaker, he also undertook some solidarity trips. They included traveling to watch some games at the historic 2010 soccer World Cup hosted by South Africa. The President traveled to support his counterpart President Jacob Zuma of South Africa at the official opening of the tournament. He also watched the Africa Cup of Nations tournament that was hosted by Angola in solidarity with Zambia's western neighbour.

We also travelled to witness the hoisting of the flag at the birth of the new state of South Sudan in Juba. It was a new nation with plenty to learn and do. When we landed, we got stuck at the airport because the air traffic control gave us a wrong bay, which led to us being blocked for over an hour.

Some trips were prompted by purely economic reasons.

The President believed in economic diplomacy and wanted Zambia to use its international relations to promote Foreign Direct Investment (FDI) and create jobs.

One of the most successful visits was to the Peoples' Republic of China. It was a ten-day State Visit which began on February 24, 2010 at the invitation of the then Chinese President, Hu Jintao.

At the end of it, Zambia had secured financing agreements to support various project to the tune of US$1.5 billion dollars. It was during the visit that the President negotiated and concluded agreements for the construction of modern sports stadia in Lusaka.

******

While on the visit the President took some time off to visit factories and key historical and tourism attractions like the Great Wall of China. These presented the few moments of excitement and relaxation during such trips. A boat cruise if time allowed came in handy. It meant a lot of fun, food and drinks.

Foreign trips were also times for the presidential advisors to come to know and bond each other.

The State House team was picked from different sectors. Some knew each other before their appointments while other did not. So, when on a foreign trip it meant eating and drinking together and living in close proximity. At times we had to share rooms when there was not enough accommodation.

We also got to know the President better.

"Dickson loves going out," the President always said when we were done with work.

"I will release him to go and see the city."

I could then sample the nearby pubs where we could go for a drink with the Chief of Protocol, Bob Samakai, my close associate during those trips.

The security had to keep an eye on us whenever we went out for drinks in a foreign country.

******

The President was also eager to open diplomatic relations with emerging economies like Turkey. He developed a close personal relationship with President Abdullah Gul. We visited Turkey twice during President Banda's three-year tenure. During the second visit agreements for the construction of a new modern airport for Lusaka and a Turkish school were sealed. Diplomatic relations between the two countries firmed up and led to the opening of the first Turkish embassy in Zambia. Defense and security cooperation was also established and there were plans to start direct flights between Lusaka and Istanbul.

At home critics characterized these trips as a "waste of public resources." Some saw him as a 'mobile President' who spent more time in the air than in Zambia.

The issue was even tabled in parliament with a question on the cost of foreign trips. Though three questions were raised in the National Assembly on the president's trips there was no attempt at a cost-benefit analysis to measure whether or not the country was benefitting from the foreign forays.

During a trip to Nigeria for example the President managed to convince one of Africa's richest men, Aliko Dangote, to set up a cement plant in Zambia. That meant jobs and the expansion of the Zambian construction industry.

The President also brought along a number of key Zambian businessmen on these trips. During each state visit, a business forum on Zambia was organized to match-make between Zambian businessmen and foreign investors. Those that participated found the events of huge benefit.

The President himself attended the forums and participated in the discussions.

On the sidelines of most summits, the President took the opportunity to engage different bilateral and multilateral institutions. He would hold meetings with the World Bank, International Monetary Fund and UN agencies on Zambian issues.

While visiting Rome, Italy, for instance he held high-level meetings with the Director General of the Food and Agriculture Organization (FAO) on food security in Zambia.

The President seemed to love Rome.

In his tenure, we visited the "external city" more than four times and once had a refueling stopover on the way to New York for the United Nations General Assembly.

It was the only place I saw him visit shops before settling for a meal.

He converted most of us to his favorite Italian dish – *spaghetti vongole!*

At the UN, he delivered his keynote maiden speech before he hosted a Zambia Business Forum. It was well attended by US investors.

After a short stint in the US, he flew on to Venezuela where he was invited by the late President Hugo Chavez to attend the Second Africa-South America (ASA) summit

It was held on the Island of Margarita and here the President made an substantial impact.

He developed cordial relation with then Brazilian President Luiz Inacio Lula da Silva. President da Silva was to visit Zambia during Banda's tenure.

The President left Venezuela for Cuba to fulfill an invitation from President Raul Castro. He clinched an agreement for the eradication of malaria in Zambia and obtained medical aid in the form of doctors who were in short supply back home.

The visit was a success.

But the cry back home was that he was spending too much time away.

Newspaper editorials criticized the trips and called on the President to return home and concentrate on solving national issues.

"I trust you had fruitful visits to the UN, Venezuela and Cuba with the President. In the light of public sentiments that the President travels too much, would it not be a good idea to advise him to brief the nation whenever he returns from any trip?" a media colleague wrote to me on October 8, 2009.

The President always traveled with a press crew to cover his foreign trips. At the end of each trip, he had a chat with the reporters and explained the results.

But there was a view that he needed to hold a full briefing on his return. I was not convinced that this would be the right way to deal with the criticism.

There was a feeling even internally that we needed to cut down on foreign trips but it was not easy as some were very crucial.

Whenever there was such a trip, I tried to issue a comprehensive statement to explain it and the possible benefits to Zambia.

The Foreign Ministry also provided some background to help the public appreciate the engagements.

I devised another method of explaining the president's trips. Initially, only journalists working for the state-run media accompanied the president. I proposed to the President that we should include the private media on the trips. He agreed.

That helped a lot. We were getting full coverage in the private media, which used to be critical of the trips.

In Egypt, I carried a full press corp.

This trip became the president's homecoming of sorts. He had started his diplomatic career as Ambassador to Cairo. He was returning to his second home only this time as head of state.

The State Visit was at the invitation of President Hosni Mubarak. There was a carnival atmosphere in Cairo when the President arrived. He was received with full military honours and the main newspapers gave him front-page coverage.

We had lunch with President Mubarak and his family at his official residence after the official talks between the two leaders. Little did we know that President Banda would be the last President to meet Mubarak in that presidential palace. A few days after the visit, Mubarak was toppled in what came to be known as the Arab spring revolution that spread rapidly in North Africa.

From that visit, Egyptair, the national airline launched direct flights into Lusaka while the Arab Contractors acquired land in Zambia to build an ultramodern housing complex.

On these visits the press crew travelled ahead of the President.

They did background stories on the country he was about to visit.

But they always faced problems in Libya, a closed country then with a minimum of media freedom. The advance press crew for instance could not film buildings because of restrictions.

We visited Libya thrice for talks with the "brother leader" Muammar Ghadaffi. He was interesting.

He dressed in traditional Arabic robes, spoke continuously but inaudibly through an interpreter. You had to listen attentively to follow the interpreter who always sat next to the brother leader.

After a seven-hour flight in the presidential jet from Lusaka to Tripoli, a long road journey always awaited us. The brother leader was never in town. We always followed him into the desert up to 200 kms where he had pitched a huge tent, surrounded by heavily armed guards and camels.

Meetings took place near a bonfire.

From the Libyan trips, we managed to get donations of tractors for small-scale farmers. Many farmers across the country benefited. Ghadaffi considered himself the leader of Africa and openly spoke ill of African Presidents who dared to challenge his hegemony.

"I will remove them one by one," he once told us, amidst laughter from our delegation.

In the year 2010, the President visited 15 countries equivalent to travelling each month. The criticism continued. But I believed most of these trips were not in vain. We achieved a lot for the country and the African region.

CHAPTER NINE
HELPING THE IVORIANS

The diplomatic skills of the President were required to help rally regional support in Southern Africa for the Ivorian President-elect Alassane Ouattara. The new Ivorian President was holed up in the now famous Hotel du Golf in Abidjan following the refusal of the incumbent Laurent Gbagbo to accept the results of the November 28, 2010 presidential election which Ouattara won.

The Ivorian Prime Minister Guillaume Soro landed in Lusaka January 25, 2011. Through diplomatic channels, the Ouattara camp had managed to reach the President and asked for an urgent appointment, which was granted.

Soro was the leader of the delegation which comprised Toikeusse Mabri, the leader of the Union for Democracy and Peace in Ivory Coast (UDPCI) which was part of the coalition formed by Ouattara. He had also been a minister in Ouattara's government during the transition. Mamadou Diane, a diplomatic advisor, was also in the delegation.

He was on a mission.

"We need the support of Zambia," the youthful prime minister told the President at State House.

I was to coordinate the assignment.

"Help your friend. He is young like you, the future belongs to you young people," the President said when introducing me to then 38 year-old premier.

Gbagbo had strong allies in Southern Africa.

The regional powerhouse South Africa and Angola remained solidly behind him even in defeat. The Ouattara camp, on the other hand, looked to Zambia for help to secure support in the region.

During his meetings with the President, Soro narrated the events leading to the disputed elections. The story was very touching as he talked of the many who had been maimed in the post–election violence. By his estimate up to the time he met with the President about 300 civilians had died, many more were internally displaced while thousands had fled the country. As the conflict escalated, international NGOs put the death toll at 3,000.

"We need to stop Gbagbo and his army from killing innocent people," Soro said.

As he was giving the brief, the President looked unsettled. He signaled me to walk to where he was seated.

"Please make sure there is food for our guests. They have come a long way," he said.

Such was his concern when meeting guests. He always wanted them to be comfortable and specifically have food before leaving State House.

After the meeting, I issued a press statement on the closed-door discussions and gave a few interviews to foreign media on Zambia's position on the situation in the Ivory Coast.

"The president's position is that Gbagbo must cede power to the winner of the November presidential elections," I said.

The visiting Prime Minister was the former leader of the New Forces rebels who were at the centre of the September 19, 2002 failed coup d'état that escalated into a brutal civil war that only ended with a peace accord in 2007. This accord propelled Soro to the position of Prime Minister.

A former student leader, he had served as Minister of Reconstruction and Reintegration as well as Minister of Communications before he was named Premier.

"Please help us restore democracy in Ivory Coast," he said almost in tears.

President-elect Ouattara had run out of food at the hotel where he was holed up and communication with the hotel was erratic. It was surrounded by heavily armed soldiers loyal to Gbagbo who did not allow anyone to leave the premises.

UN peacekeepers had been deployed to protect the leaders who were inside the hotel. The UN helicopters were the only means of bringing in supplies including food to the hotel and facilitate the movement out of Ouattara's closest allies like Soro.

After listening to Soro, the President decided that the Zambian Prime Minister should personally go and present the same facts to other leaders in the region. The President further tasked Foreign Minister Kabinga Pande to coordinate a Southern region response to the Ivory Coast situation. The Zambian minister joined the Soro delegation to assist in making contact with other foreign ministers in the region.

"Let's talk to our friends," the President said.

He also telephoned fellow presidents in SADC to rally support for Ouattara. The President had very good personal relations with his South African counterpart, Jacob Zuma.

Within a few minutes of these events, the plane took off from the Lusaka International Airport. On board was the Zambian foreign minister with the Ivorian premier on a flight to South Africa to meet the authorities there. A Zambian peace initiative was taking shape.

Following several consultations, South Africa softened her position on the situation in Ivory Coast. Angola also did the same with the foreign minister issuing the first anti-Gbagbo statement.

The *Guardian* newspaper of the United Kingdom published a story on April 5, 2011, titled "Laurent Gbagbo, alone and shunned by African leaders". The story indicated that Angola, his last ally had changed position and backed his removal.

Gbagbo was isolated and remained vulnerable while stuck in the Presidential palace.

The President tasked me to help the Ivorian Prime Minister in whatever way I could during his stay in Lusaka. I kept constant touch with his team who stayed at the five-star Pamodzi Hotel in Lusaka.

I pitched several stories for the Prime Minister with various international newspapers through his press aide Meite Sindou. He made news by putting pressure on Gbagbo from Lusaka.

The support we gave to the Ivorian group was well-received by many Zambians, including critics of the President. It was appropriate, they said.

I worked with the Prime Minister and his press aide to put together a press conference the day before he left Zambia after a four-day visit.

Soro spoke English but preferred to use French at the press briefing.

"I am more comfortable in French," he said.

I organized for an interpreter for the event. But when reporters pressed him with questions, he resorted to English, speaking articulately on the issues. He made a good impression.

Some local radio stations gave the conference live coverage.

"Gbagbo must go. We are not prepared to see any more innocent civilians die or run to other countries because of one person. We will use all possible means including a targeted military operation to force this dictator to give up power" he said.

He commended the initiative by President Banda of trying to help resolve the crisis through engaging the leaders of the Southern African region.

President Banda's strategy on the matter was to lobby SADC members to support the position taken by the Economic Community of West African States (Ecowas), the regional economic bloc for West African countries.

Ecowas had suspended Ivory Coast's membership and demanded that Gbagbo cede power to the internationally recognized winner Ouattara. Ecowas was working in close consultation with the African Union (AU).

"We have been assured by the Zambian President that Zambia will closely follow events in Cote D'ivoire and that he will follow up the decision of the AU as one of his priorities," Soro said.

The President asked me to organize for food to be airlifted to Ivory Coast to help the President-elect and his team at the hotel. This is after Prime Minister told us that he had a way of getting the food to the President-elect.

I organized several cooler boxes of beef, which the premier carried on his plane on his way back.

******

While in Zambia, the President felt sorry for the young premier.

"He must be bored just sitting in the hotel. Does he go out?" he asked.

"No sir, he is always busy I think," I answered.

The President was very concerned with the Prime Minister's situation as he remained in the hotel throughout. He regularly called me to check on the Prime Minister's condition.

By that time the Prime Minister looked stressed and exhausted. He had been having meetings, interviews and traveling in the region almost on a daily basis without enough rest.

The President decided that we should try and make the Prime Minister's stay in Zambia worthwhile.

Inside the Presidency

"Organize a trip for him to visit other towns of Zambia. He needs a breather," the President said.

After consultations with his team, it was agreed that he would visit the North-Western provincial capital of Solwezi and the nearby Kansanshi Mine and possibly spend a quiet afternoon at the luxurious golf course.

The Zambia Air Force Presidential plane was put on the mission.

When he was about to leave for the airport however, he got seriously ill. His blood pressure just shot up and he felt dizzy.

The President panicked and dispatched his personal doctor to check on the Prime Minister. He needed treatment and the trip was aborted.

"I really feel bad about the situation in Ivory Coast," the President said.

He told us that we should be prepared to leave State House should he lose the elections that year saying a country was more important than personal interests.

"There is more to life than being President," he would say occasionally.

******

After a four months standoff and of political deadlock, Gbagbo was forcibly removed from the Presidential palace by soldiers loyal to Ouattara, backed by the UN and French troops, who stormed the bunker where he hid. In the processhe was arrested and taken into custody. Pictures of the dejected former President, wearing a vest and an open shirt, as he was led off, were splashed around the world.

The Associated Press quoted a pro-Ouattara soldier, Issard Soumahro who participated in the raid, as saying Gbagbo was hiding in the bunker when they stormed the Presidential palace.

"He was there with his wife and son. He wasn't hurt but he was tired and his cheek was swollen after a soldier slapped him," read the dispatch of April 11, 2011.

The former President was later that year transferred to the International Criminal Court (ICC) in The Hague in advance of being charged for crimes committed during the post-election violence. He was due to be tried by the ICC.

At the end of the standoff, over 3,000 civilians had been reported killed in the unrest.

******

When the Prime Minister was leaving Zambia, the Ivorian delegation thought I should be rewarded for the extra work I did in helping them to secure appointments, interviews and organize a press conference.

"No thank you, it is the President's contribution to the struggle," I said.

They appeared surprised.

"We didn't realize Zambians were such nice people," an aide said.

******

The ousting of Gbagbo facilitated the President-elect's inauguration as President of Ivory Coast.

Ouattara invited President Banda to attend the swearing in ceremony on May 6, 2011 but he could not make it. The President instead dispatched his Vice President George Kunda to represent the country. The new Ivorian leadership was happy with the role Zambia played.

Soro was later elected Member of Parliament in his hometown of Boundiali and consecutively Speaker of Ivory Coast's Parliament.

CHAPTER TEN
THE PRESIDENT'S HATCHET MAN

My job at State House put me in the spotlight but also in the firing line.

I was quoted in the media almost every day speaking on behalf of the President. I announced dismissals and appointments on behalf of the administration. I was the centre of attraction. Some admired me but some others viewed me with distaste.

I was considered by some to be the President's hatchet man. One article described me as "a resident evil" while I was also called a "bad boy". Others plotted my downfall.

I was considered to be too close to the President and some believed I misled him on a number of issues. The attacks came from different angles even from within State House. They were unbearable at times!

Fake intelligence reports reached the President about my conduct: I was not suitable for the job. I was too young. I was spending too much time in bars smoking Cuban Cigars and drinking single malt whiskies.

"You have to be careful the way you carry yourself in public," the President warned me after he showed me a report detailing my conduct.

It was largely composed of falsehoods.

"I know these are lies but be careful. Not everyone is happy with your appointment," he said in a fatherly way.

At State House, some of my colleagues thought I was meddling in their jobs. I had become an all-rounder, dealing with everything else when my job was press and public relations, they alleged.

Some cabinet ministers thought I was the President's political bruiser who fed him with all sorts of stories to satisfy a political agenda.

One minister even upset the President when he tried to raise the issue of my alleged infidelity.

"I don't believe in gossip, we have serious national issues to deal with," the President said in response to the allegation.

My enemies increased with time and attempts to drive a wedge between me and the President failed. I remained his trusted confidant on many issues.

Some of my foes took the fight public.

Senior party officials fired the first shot against me.

The governing party was facing internal problems. Morale in the party was at the lowest it had ever been and some senior party officials resigned citing poor leadership.

A retreat was organized for officials to discuss the internal party problems and map out the way forward. Some participants at that retreat noted that the President was not spending enough time on party matters. They alleged that State House aides had confined the President to government duties at the expense of party affairs.

I was singled out as the major stumbling block to the smoothening relations between the party and the President. I was also not helping improve the image of the President, they added.

"What is Dickson Jere doing to raise the public image of the President?" one official was quoted by the press as having said at the end of the retreat.

Others opined that I should be removed from State House.

The *Post* carried a story on the outcome of the retreat under the headline: "The MMD is in serious trouble." It was reported that I was to be blame for the poor relations between the President and the party, and that I was blocking appointments between the President and party members.

I was never given an opportunity to present my side of the story.

If those accusing me had bothered to check, they would have realized that it was not my role to plan the President's diary. Others had that responsibility. In fact, at times I equally had to fight to put my programmes on the diary.

The President was not happy with the stories that were published after the retreat and in particular the attacks on me. He always took such as attacks as being on him.

"If anyone has problems with my staff, they should approach me. I can't allow this kind of behaviour," he said.

The privately held daily, *The Post*, that was consistently critical of the President gave me rare support in one editorial. Throughout, they had been hard on the President and me but not this time.

"Blaming a young man like Dickson for Rupiah's problems is nonsense. All those blaming Dickson for Rupiah's problems are simply cowards who can't go and tell Rupiah that his performance is very poor," read the November 22, 2009 editorial in part.

"Mealy-mouthed shedding of responsibility and blaming it all on Dickson and others around Rupiah is, at best, hypocrisy and, at worst, a form of dishonesty," the editorial continued.

I don't know how the newspaper decided to defend me because they had previously, an editorial, described me as "an empty head" that was misleading the President.

The Post story on the retreat was just the beginning of more attacks on me.

Soon after the retreat, my secretary alerted me to a story in the press about me. It alleged that was abusing the presidential intelligence information to supposedly fix my political enemies. The story appeared on the online publication, *Zambian Watchdog,* and quoted senior intelligence officers as saying that they were not happy with my unhindered access to confidential intelligence files for the President.

I realized the fight was getting bigger and nastier.

I was accused of working with a clique of ministers who were close to the President to sort out those we thought were 'threats to our positions' at State House.

"Mr. Jere, you must have very powerful enemies," said Richard Sakala, who had served in my position as spokesman for Zambia's second President Frederick Chiluba.

"But you are lucky that they don't know how State House operates," he added when he called me after he read the story.

The fact was that nobody could access intelligence reports without the consent of the President. The reports go directly to the President and are shredded after they are read. One could only access them if the President himself showed them to you.

I ignored the story although I made a copy for the President. I always notified him of such. It was good to keep him informed on the shenanigans that were going on.

******

While on a trip with the President, a story popped up on my blackberry. I had activated the Google alert that immediately notified me when there was a story published on the President or me.

"RB upset with Dickson Jere for acquiring property using his name," the headline screamed.

In the story, I was accused of having corruptly purchased a 250 acre farm for a cash consideration of US$100,000 in my hometown of Chipata in Eastern Zambia. According to the story, I forced the elderly owner of the farm to sell it to me. The farm was right next to the President's.

"Where did he get such kind of money?" the story, which was first published on *Zambian Watchdog* asked.

It was a big story. It circulated fast on the Internet blogs.

But it died down quietly after the local branch of Transparency International independently checked the veracity of the story and found it to have been a fabrication.

"People must really hate you for them to create such a story...," said Goodwell Lungu, Executive Director of anti-corruption watchdog.

He had called to inform me that their findings showed I was clean.

It is true that I had purchased farmland in Chipata through a government loan. But it was not next to the President's farm. The President was aware of the transaction because I kept him informed as was my practice. Indeed, he was the one who encouraged me to get land in Chipata.

The press was on me for a comment.

"My comment on this matter is no comment," I would answer.

The President, of course, ignored the story. He knew it was false.

But just around that same time, a report reached the President that alleged that, when we got drunk, I and his eldest son James were throwing cash to whoever was at Portico, an Italian Bar in Lusaka that we patronized.

Even though it was a fabrication, it upset the President!

"This is getting out of hand now...," he said visibly angry.

This was the first time that the President was really angry with me. He had advised me to stay away from public drinking places. So why was I at the Italian club?

******

Just when the President was cooling down, I did something impulsive. I ordered the prison authorities to release a family friend who was on the verge of death.

I acted on emotions because his family had called me for help after they received news that Xavier Franklin Chungu, the former intelligence chief, who was in jail on corruption charges, needed urgent medical attention. I ordered that he be moved to a government hospital under guard.

After my instructions were carried out, I reported to the President at about 05:00 hours.

I woke him up with my early morning call.

"What has happened to call me at such an ungodly hour," he asked.

My decision riled the system.

Later that day, a special meeting of security and senior government officials was convened to deal with me. In attendance was the State House Chief of Staff. I had no powers to order the release of a prisoner and I was told that in no uncertain terms.

I opted to remain silent throughout the proceedings. I knew I did something wrong and impulsive but for the right reasons.

When pictures of Chungu were received by the President, he almost broke down when he saw the huge stitches on his stomach.

"I understand why you acted that way," he told me two weeks after the incident.

That week, I travelled with him to Mfuwe, the gateway to the South Luangwa National Park where he was due to meet President Joseph Kabila of the Democratic Republic of the Congo.

Usually, we took a plane and a chopper would be on standby at the airport.

After the talks, I briefed the press on the outcome before driving to the airport.

Suddenly, the programme changed.

The President was not coming with us to Lusaka. He had a family engagement at his farm in Chipata. We were not required to be with him.

He pulled me aside as I was about to board the plane.

"You take my chopper," he said in a low voice.

With other State House officials we flew on the presidential chopper to Lusaka on the clear instructions of the President.

But the story was subsequently twisted.

I commandeered the presidential helicopter for a jolly-ride with friends, the story alleged. It added that I went to watch wild animals in the National Park without the knowledge of the President. When

I returned to Lusaka, I landed at the State House helipad reserved for the President, drunk while holding a bottle of Blue Label whisky, it said.

Someone within our circle had leaked the same story to local journalists.

The press was on me to verify the information they had received. But after I explained to them, they dropped the story because they realized it was false.

It is instructive that I was the only one singled out when the other passengers were also presidential staff.

"When there is a problem at State House, DJ's (Dickson Jere) name is always mentioned even when he was not around," said Robinson Nkonde, the senior private secretary to the President.

"Your name seems to always attract trouble," he would often say.

******

The stories were slowly taking a toll on me.

My job was to protect the image of the President but now it was my image that needed to be protected.

I remembered the words of British Prime Minister David Cameroon's spin-doctor Andy Coulson when he said: "When a spokesman needs a spokesman, it's time to move on".

Deep down my heart, I thought I should probably move on like Coulson did when he was embroiled in the telephone hacking scandal that overshadowed his role as spokesman forcing him to resign his job on January 21, 2011.

After much contemplation, I decided to stay the course. After all, my relationship with the President remained sound.

When the President travelled to New York, I got permission to go in advance with a commercial airline. I flew from Lusaka to London where I made a brief stopover to attend to personal issues. I was to join the New York delegation later.

My phone beeped. It was a Google alert.

Gosh, what now? Am I in the news again?

I scrolled the smartphone and yes, it was a story on me again!

It claimed that I had ejected a female photojournalist, Emma Nakapizye, from the President's delegation in New York because I was not happy with the manner she was covering the President and his family.

Inside the Presidency

The story perplexed me to say the least. I was in London and not New York.

So when she was being put on the next flight back home, I was not even there.

I quickly telephoned the Ministry of Information officials who were responsible for reporters working for government. I was told the journalist was recalled because she had taken someone else's slot.

The incident generated a fair amount of heat. Media watchdog organizations held protests against me, including a joint statement condemning "Dickson Jere's unbecoming behaviour" even though I was not privy to the incident in New York. The statement, signed by colleagues I had worked with, was very harsh on me.

I was the bad person who was harassing the journalists.

"I am in London and not New York," I let them know.

They were surprised because someone told them I chaired the "ejection" meeting in New York.

"Check your facts before you issue statements," I told them.

When we returned to Lusaka, I wanted to take some days off and reflect on some of those developments but the President would have none of it.

"You have to be strong..." he said when encouraging me to soldier on.

"I get insulted everyday but don't feel like quitting," he said and it was true that he was attacked almost every day in the media but often he ignored the negative stories.

"They will get tired," he used to say after reading a negative story on him.

While trying to settle down following the increasing negative stories, I was back in the media with another negative story.

I realized I just had to live with them and that was to be my life at State House.

****

While in Chipata with the President, unruly MMD supporters pounced on a photojournalist from *The Post* newspaper. He was talking to me when the incident started at the airport. I of course, rescued the journalist.

But the following day, the newspaper published a picture of the reporter being beaten by the party supporters while I was sandwiched in between.

A letter of complaint was written to the President to take action.

It landed on my desk and without consulting the President I responded saying the incident was unfortunate and pledged to protect the press from harassment in future.

It was my job to make sure reporters covering the President were not harassed.

"We are not sure if Rupiah dictated this letter to Dickson or Dickson just used his initiative to deal with the situation. We say this because the letter is full of contradictions and blatant lies," an editorial in the *The Post* read.

They, once again, showed the picture of me with the thugs beating the reporter saying I knew the people who attacked the journalist.

I worked with the security agencies to make sure that such ugly incidents were avoided in future.

******

The President was furious.

He summoned senior staff for an emergency meeting. He had received reports that someone among us was clearing aircrafts to land or overfly the Zambian airspace in the night. He had given nobody such permission and the clearance was done without his knowledge. The security system was worried about the trend.

The source, had mentioned my name as among the suspects.

During the tense meeting, one of us owned up and apologized.

"Your name was on the list," the President's senior private secretary told me days after the meeting.

The president's usual counsel followed. I should be careful with whatever I did because I was in the spotlight.

The *Zambian Watchdog* carried other damning stories about me and other State House staff. By then, I had grown a thick skin not to be bothered with such.

One such story, which widely circulated, was titled; "President Banda's thieving son and corrupt drunkards who run State House".

It was a narrative of falsehoods about me and others of receiving bribes from businessmen to facilitate appointments with the President. The story described me as one who had emerged from "zero to hero" through my political connections and illegal deals.

Silence, I learnt, was golden at such times.

One day I received a telephone call from my worker at my smallholding in Lusaka's Lilayi area. My farm had been invaded by party youths who started sharing the land among themselves. It was an act of impunity to say the least.

The only offence I committed was to issue a statement on behalf of the President directing the police to arrest anyone found grabbing idle land regardless of their political affiliation. At that time, I received a complaint from lawyer Wynter Kabimba, a senior opposition official, who complained of MMD cadres that had grabbed farmland belonging to his client.

"We want to teach him a lesson," they told my hapless worker as they moved on my farm.

I mobilized police and rushed to the scene to disperse them.

The President got the news and was livid.

"This anarchy must stop. If they think Dickson has done something wrong, is this the way of punishing him?" the President asked.

He summoned the entire security and defence command where he gave strict orders that land that had been taken by party members should be reverted to the owners forthwith.

"This is a country of laws," he said and announced a special taskforce to tackle the land grabbing problem by party zealots.

The President's intervention made me an enemy of the party youths.

"He is a bad boy," they often said about me.

Other issues that put me in bad books with friends and relatives was my usual reluctance to use my position to influence awards of government contracts or jobs. I thought it was not appropriate to interfere with such processes in government institutions. In my view, it would amount to abuse of office.

"He is in State House and yet can't get us jobs in government," one relative often said.

In fact most of the complaints came from those who were ill-qualified for the advertised jobs.

******

But in the midst of all this, I had friends as well who supported me throughout the challenging periods. The Secretary to the Cabinet Dr. Joshua Kanganja and his deputy Robert Mataka provided me with valuable counsel. They guided me on the civil service rules, regulations and on how to take certain decisions. I survived partly because of their wise counsel.

"My dear, don't respond to that issue. We shall handle it from here," Kanganja would say.

I had worked with both of them at the Constitution Review Commission. And, possibly, due to this interaction and bonding they were ready to help.

By the end of Banda's tenure, I was still his spokesman. I even got promoted from the position of Chief Policy Analyst to Special Assistant to the President for Press and Public Relations – the post was at the level of deputy secretary to the Cabinet- the second highest in the civil service.

I survived the political shenanigans and lived to tell the tale.

CHAPTER ELEVEN
"THE COOKIE IS CRUMBLING"

I was summoned by Zambia's second President Frederick Chiluba.

"It's urgent," he said on the telephone.

I sought permission from the President who gave me the green light to meet the founding leader of the governing party.

He had concerns over the way the President was handling governance issues.

He thought Mr. Banda was too lenient on erring government and party officials.

When I reached his Kabulonga home in Lusaka, I found him seated by the poolside alone reading a big King James Version of the Holy Bible. He was a small-bodied man and about 5 feet tall.

"Dick, what's going on?" he asked without elaborating as he pointed to a chair next to him.

He looked tense.

"Why is everyone resigning?" he asked a second question before I could answer. He offered me a soft drink.

The Deputy Minister for Works and Supply Lameck Mangani had just resigned from government and the governing party. He used to be a close-ally of the President and was a putative relative. He had served as minister of home affairs before he was demoted to deputy minister.

The resignation shocked many.

"Please tell the President to act now! Let him not allow the impression to be created that the cookie is crumbling," Chiluba said, bluntly.

The former President, who called himself a political engineer, gave me a long political lecture. He spoke non-stop mainly on the need for the President to be tough on what he said was the increasing number of dissidents in the party and government

He told me how he dissolved the entire cabinet when he was President just to instill discipline.

"These resignations are meant to weaken him. Let him sack all those he suspects to be undermining him," he said.

That was the reason he had called for me and he said I should relay the message to the President and give him feedback.

He came through as bossy, eager to give orders.

"I hear you sir, but that's not my role," I said and referred him to other colleagues who were in-charge of the politics.

"Dick, don't forget I was President before. I know how State House operates...you have the ear of the President, that I know," he said.

******

The same day, I relayed the message to the President.

He kept on nodding his head as I told him what the former President had said. When I was done, the President said that Chiluba had a point.

"But how do you just fire people without evidence?" he asked rhetorically.

He believed that no one should be dismissed without tangible evidence of wrong-doing and in some cases he preferred other sanctions even in the face of such evidence.

Defence minister George Mpombo had quit his post earlier and now Mangani. Mpombo's resignation was very unusual. In Zambia and Africa, generally, ministers rarely resign from their positions even in the face of serious allegations against them. At the time of his resignation, Mpombo was seen as a close ally of the President. He was one of the few ministers who defended the President against opposition attacks.

But a few months after he quit, he announced that he would support the opposition in the next elections because the President had failed to deliver.

A number of other senior party officials also joined the resignation bandwagon mainly citing poor leadership at the top. Among those who resigned was the one-time Minister of Lands, Judith Kapijimpanga.

The President took the resignations as a self-cleansing exercise.

******

On December 18, 2010, I received a call from the President.

It was around 18:00 hours and he wanted to see me urgently. He was at home.

I quickly got to Nkhwazi House where I found him reading through a pile of files.

"Prepare a dismissal letter," he said.

It was for the deputy Sports Minister Maynard Misapa, he told me.

He said that his information was that the minister was planning to resign that same week.

"You announce that I have relieved him of his duties," he said.

It was part of my routine to do that.

But when I got to the office to prepare the letter and news release, the President was on the line again. I should counter-check the information he had on the deputy minister, he said.

"Maybe he has been framed. I don't like firing people anyhow," he said.

I was to use my contacts to verify the information.

"Hold on to the letter and your statement," he instructed.

We verified with different security sources. The information was about 90 percent accurate. The opposition had already organized a press briefing at which the minister would announce his resignation.

"We have to announce it," I told him.

I could hear from the tone of his voice that he was not sure we should do so.

"Put yourself in his shoes. I don't want his children to suffer when I fire him for nothing," he said.

The President wanted us to be 100 percent certain, which at the time was difficult.

I devised a trap.

I invited the minister to attend a function with the President a day before his intended resignation. He showed up with his family and seemed happy to be with the President.

"This President is God-given to Zambia," he said to me that night.

The President was convinced that his political enemies had framed him.

The sources of the information, however, insisted that he was quitting the following day and that the press conference was scheduled for 10:00 hours.

I had another plan.

I invited the minister to join the President for a school visit at 08:00 hours at the American International School of Lusaka where the President's granddaughter was performing at a concert.

The minister showed up around 08:30 hours, slightly late though. Strangely, he came in a private taxi saying his official driver had not showed up that morning.

He joined the President in the public gallery where he was jovial - chanting slogans in support of the President.

"You now understand why I don't like firing people without tangible facts," the President told me after the minister had arrived.

The intelligence agencies were also on firm grounds – they insisted that the minister was due to resign at 10:00 hours. The information was impeccable, they insisted.

At 09:45 hours, the function was over.

The President thanked the minister for having accompanied him.

"Let's go and have a cup of tea at home," the President invited the minister.

We were surprised when he said that he could not make it because he had a prior engagement at 10:00 hours. Ministers relished such invitations, which came rarely and it was unusual for them to turn them down.

The alarm bells rung in the President's head. It was true the minister was resigning.

"Give him his dismissal letter," he whispered to me as he jumped into his car.

But I didn't carry the letter and asked the minister to accompany me to State House.

"I have a small parcel for you," I said.

Reluctantly, he agreed. We drove in the same vehicle and reached my office.

He suddenly started panicking. He wanted to leave for an urgent appointment.

My initial plan was to keep him longer than necessary but after I consulted the President, he told me to let him leave.

"I know you have a press conference," I told him as I handed over the letter of dismissal.

My colleague, Dr. Richard Chembe, the President's economic advisor, was called in to be my witness as I performed the task in my office.

The Minister looked disturbed. He mumbled some words to himself before apologizing to us. We didn't understand why he had to apologize.

"I am very sorry...say sorry to the President," he said to us.

My assistant had already gathered the press to announce the dismissal.

By the time the minister was going to his press briefing, the fact of his dismissal had already hit the airwaves.

He announced the resignation that same day but it was too late because we had pre-empted him.

The opposition had planned to have him address the press briefing as minister but the plot failed. When he addressed the briefing, it looked more of sour grapes because his dismissal was already announced. Even though his resignation had little impact, the opposition used the occasion to claim that many more ministers were planning to jump ship.

"This is just the tip of the iceberg, many more are coming to join us," Sata said when welcoming the minister to his party.

******

The former President Chiluba was back on the line:

"Dick, I told you the President must be tough."

This time he was blaming me for not taking his earlier advice seriously.

"I didn't just pick on you... I know you can talk straight with his Excellency," he said.

He was concerned that the resignations had continued unabated thereby weakening the President.

Meanwhile, attacks on the President from senior members of the party and some of his old friends intensified.

Within cabinet, he faced some silent resentment especially with his style of leadership, where he liked working through cabinet committees as opposed to meeting whole cabinet ministers for strategic planning. Cabinet committees were very effective in handling technical issues and, usually, carefully selected people attended such. These committees has the required competence or qualifications for such issues.

The President at times delegated the chairing of the full cabinet meetings to his Vice President George Kunda while he spent time having key meetings in the adjacent room.

"Please talk to the President to be chairing all cabinet meetings. Ministers think he is belittling them by having the Vice President, whom they don't even respect, take charge," one minister close to the President once confided in me.

The cracks in cabinet openly emerged when the President refused to allow his and ministers salaries to be increased amidst economic problems in the nation. The President asked the ministers who were not happy with his rejection of salary increments to resign.

But that only brought more anger against him from his cabinet.

"Your boss is selfish. He doesn't pay any bills like us but he refuses for us to have salary increments. It is very unfair," one minister retorted after cabinet adjourned.

******

Pressure on the President intensified.

One of the founder members of the governing party Mbita Chitala openly supported the opposition saying the President had failed to deliver on his mandate. It is noteworthy that Mbita Chitala was in charge of the President's Campaign Centre in 2008.

Even some of the opposition leaders that supported the President's candidature in the 2008 presidential by-election now switched allegiance and started attacking. In the private media, leaders with virtually no political following were given front-page coverage in order to show that the ruling party was collapsing. It was getting nasty. Every day, newspapers had a new person joining in the attack. It was a well planned and executed political ploy.

The former President decided to throw his hat into the ring.

He called a press conference on February 21, 2010 where he attacked the opposition and those in government whom he said were "stifling progress" by undermining the President.

"My unqualified support for President Rupiah Banda is based on my personal judgment and assessment of the man," he told reporters.

"I am impressed that he is capable of re-uniting our nation, bring development to all parts of Zambia, give every Zambian equal opportunity and of course promote equality of treatment," the former President said.

He pledged his unwavering support to the President.

He was an orator and his speech was widely covered in the press.

"I have opened the floodgates, its over to you now," Chiluba said when I telephoned him to thank him for coming to the rescue of the President.

The divisions in government and the party widened.

There were officials who thought that the President had allowed newcomers to hijack the party. Others thought the party was not looking after its members by not awarding them business contracts in government.

Some senior officials were trading insults in the media.

The President had to take some measures, although belatedly, in order to restore sanity and bring back harmony in the party. He dismissed the Minister of Works and Supply, Mike Mulongoti, who was at loggerheads with the country's Vice-President George Kunda. The two were attacking each other in the press ahead of party elections in which both aspired for the number two position.

"I have therefore decided to relieve him of his duties as minister and I have revoked his nomination as Member of Parliament with immediate effect," the President told a news briefing.

"He has openly ridiculed the Vice President claiming that he was far much better than him. I am compelled to act in the interests of the party and the government in order to preserve unity and maintain discipline," he said.

Mulongoti blamed Chiluba for his dismissal.

He later joined the opposition and attacked the President throughout the campaign period.

Before Mulongoti, the President had only sacked one minister and two deputy ministers. Gabriel Namulambe, Minister of Science, Technology and Vocational Training was sacked for publicly supporting tribalism and attacking the President in the press but was later brought back as deputy Minister after he apologized. The two deputy ministers were Jonas Shakafuswa and Lameck Chibombamilimo for Science, Technology and Vocational Training and Energy and Water Development respectively.

Later the President sacked another deputy Minister Chrispin Musosha for indiscipline. The President had insisted that I should mention in the statement that he was sacked as part of instilling discipline and order in the government and party.

"The President said he has decided to relieve Musosha of his duties because of indiscipline and causing wrangles in government and the MMD," I said in the statement.

"The President said discipline in his government is very paramount and that all Ministers, Deputy Ministers, Members of Parliament and party officials should at all times adhere to good behaviour," I said.

Dr. Solomon Musonda lost his ministerial job after he was arrested in connection with a criminal charge. He was accused of having shot a member of an opposition party.

Still, the situation within the party remained volatile.

The party provincial committees were required to elect fresh office bearers. Almost all incumbents were facing tough battles from new entrants.

The former President called again.

This time he summoned me and my buddy, James, the son of the President to meet him.

James was helping the party with fundraising.

"Tell the President to allow new people to takeover leadership at provincial level," he said.

The old leadership should be replaced because they had overstayed. The party machinery needed oiling in readiness for the 2011 general elections.

"New leaders will be eager to deliver than the old ones," Chiluba said, citing his experiences in the 1996 elections when he won a second term in office.

He suggested that the current chairpersons should be assigned other duties either in government or the party to pave way for fresh blood.

We agreed with the former President's reasoning. We delivered the message but the President did not agree entirely.

"It's payback time," he told us.

"We are here (State House) because of the provincial leaders who voted unanimously for my nomination in 2008," he said.

The provincial leaders formed part of the national executive committee of the party, which made up the Electoral College for picking the presidential candidate.

That was the character of the President. He always remembered those who played a role in his election as the Presidential candidate of the party and as President of the country later. He treasured loyalty.

He said he was going to back every serving chairperson for re-election unless they opted out.

But on the ground, the serving leaders were unpopular. The President was going against the tide.

It took the President's intervention for some to win while others went unopposed after opponents were talked out of the race. It was a very difficult assignment to carry out. I was among those tasked to handle the negotiations together with other senior party officials.

At times, the President himself took up the assignment.

"I am not pulling out of the race," said Chishala Chilufya, a populist candidate vying for the Eastern Province.

I was tasked to deal with him since he was a friend.

"It's democracy. I am not pulling out," he told me.

I shuttled between different camps trying to find a solution.

"Young man you have been thrown into the deep end," said Vernon Mwaanga, a veteran politician we traveled with on the mission.

He was referring to my involvement in the tense process.

Eastern province was the hottest.

It was the home area of the President and party members disagreed with him on the choice of leadership.

"Mr. Jere, you tell the President the truth, if he picks someone else here, we will not support his candidate," they would openly say.

It was equally my home area and I knew most of them on a personal level.

Members from the party branch wanted the current crop to go.

Negotiations took us to midnight.

A truce was only achieved the following morning barely hours before voting.

At the end of the nine provincial elections, almost all old leaders were retained -courtesy of the President. But the morale in the party structures took a hit. It was low. In some cases, there were resignations.

The opposition relished such news. The private media splashed stories of the party bigwigs who had quit in protest against what they called 'imposition of candidates'.

Was the cookie crumbling? I thought of the former President's words when I read the stories on the political fallout within the ruling party.

CHAPTER TWELVE

"WHERE THERE IS HATRED LET ME BRING LOVE"

The President made a political jibe meant for one wayward Roman Catholic priest but it inadvertently angered the Roman Catholic Church in Zambia.

At a news conference in Kitwe, he referred to Father Frank Bwalya as a father with no children.

"There is that other man who has no children but is called a Father. He is not even a Catholic Father anymore" he said in his off-the-cuff remarks on April 20, 2010.

Fr. Bwalya had launched a political campaign against the President using the Catholic-owned *Radio Icengelo* in Kitwe, a mining town north of Lusaka.

The President's remark did not go down well among the Catholic faithful. They are an influential group in Zambia, with a membership of around one third of the population.

The blame was heaped on me.

"Why did you allow such a thing to happen?" a Catholic priest I knew asked in an email.

"Find a way of asking the President to apologize."

Those of us who attended the briefing understood the context and most took it as a lighthearted remark.

But *The Post* newspaper edition of April 24, 2010 reported it under the emotive headline: "*Banda has no respect for Catholic Church.*"

Many Catholics were upset.

"I think it is an insult on the Catholic priests," said Simon Kabanda, a devout Catholic and Executive Director of the NGO, Citizens' Forum.

"He has no respect for the Catholic Church," he said and some priests joined in the condemnation.

At the time relations between the Catholic Church and Government were frosty. The Chief government spokesman, Information Minister

Lt-General Ronnie Shikapwasha called the Catholics 'genocidal" in reference to the alleged role of some priests in the 1994 Rwanda genocide.

The accusation riled the Catholics.

The Church leadership demanded an apology from government and the Bishops met the President over the minister's remark.

But instead of apologizing, Gen. Shikapwasha challenged the Catholics to deny that they had a role in the genocide, which merely exacerbated matters.

The Minister, who was a Reverend in the Pentecostal Church, further accused the Catholic priests of inciting civil strife in Zambia by issuing "reckless political statements."

At that time senior government officials were involved in lengthy discussions with the church leadership over the conduct of their priests and Father Bwalya in particular.

We in government thought the cleric was abusing his priestly duties by rallying support for the opposition using the Church radio. We considered his radio programmes to be part of the opposition's effort to incite people to rise against the government.

Once, the police stormed the studios and arrested the vocal priest who at the time was saying that the President was illegitimate because he had rigged the 2008 presidential by-election.

We engaged the Vatican ambassador Archbishop Nicola Girasoli on the matter. He was sympathetic to government concerns and agreed that the priest's behaviour was not what it should have been.

"You need to raise the issue with the Bishop in-charge of his diocese," he advised.

He also tried to quietly resolve the issue by engaging the bishops.

The Bishop of the Ndola Diocese was Noel O'regan. His office was "swamped" by government officials who wanted to discuss the political activities of his priest and I was one of those who met him.

After several meetings, the Bishop acted to our satisfaction.

He convinced the priest to go on a year's sabbatical and relinquish his position as the radio's station manager and priest of the Ipusukilo Parish.

"He was removed because we wanted to clear the air over some of his personal views that did not represent the Church's position but were being said in his personal capacity," the Bishop said on a live radio programme.

"I have approved the application from Father Bwalya to go on sabbatical," he said and added that the priest was now free to speak on national issues.

That's how the priest left the Church and formed the NGO *Change Life Zambia*, which worked with the opposition against the President and the governing party. They held joint political rallies mainly in the Copperbelt.

"The government thought by removing me from *Radio Icengelo* and eliminating my voice from the airwaves of this community radio they had succeeded in shutting me up. They were mistaken," he said on April 30, 2010, which marked his first anniversary outside active priesthood.

He worked with a number of young Catholic priests even when he was on sabbatical in his campaigns.

He was dubbed 'John the Baptist' while others called him "Aristide" in reference to the former Catholic priest, Jean-Bertrand Aristide, who became President of Haiti.

******

With the controversial priest out of the way, government and the Church tried to mend relations.

The President met the bishops during the annual conference of the Zambia Episcopal Conference (ZEC) and was special guest at the installation of Catholic Bishops at the invitation of the Church. His first engagement was at the ordination of Bishop Alick Banda, who became the first Zambian to be Bishop of Ndola on February 13, 2010.

The President used the occasion to speak on Church-government relations.

"My government will listen to the Church. I personally believe that this form of constructive engagement with the Church is healthy for the development of our nation," he said.

"What is improper, however, is the tendency by some members of the clergy to personalize their disagreement with government and begin to attack individuals in the media especially myself," he told the gathering.

He later attended the installation of Monsignor Benjamin Phiri as Auxiliary Bishop of Chipata and later the ordination of Monsignor Charles Kasonde as Bishop of Solwezi. He then officiated at the consecration of Bishop Evans Chinyemba who was installed as Bishop of Mongu following the retirement of Bishop Duffy.

It appeared that a thaw was being achieved.

However, some priests did not appear to be ready for reconciliation.. Father Miha Drevensek, a Slovenian, who was head of Mission Press and a strong critic of the President, said that the perceived reconciliation could not work because it was not genuine.

"Shikapwasha said we Catholics will cause genocide in the country. President Banda should get rid of Shikapwasha if reconciliation is to be regarded genuine," he said.

Attacks from individual priests continued unabated. Nearly every week, one priest or the other would be quoted in the media attacking the President and government.

Bishop Paul Duffy, the octogenarian American priest, who was in-charge of western Zambia, was a fierce critic of the President and the government.

"You know I have said here in Western Province it seems that people think it's time for change," he said in one of the many interviews he gave.

The President decided to engage him directly and they met for the first time during a presidential visit at the President's request.

We drove to the Bishop's residence where we were warmly received.

He looked surprised by the arrival of the presidential entourage at his modest home. When he was told by his staff earlier that the President wanted to see him, he thought it was a joke.

"I have never been visited by a President before," he said.

He had been in Zambia for many years.

After exchanging some pleasantries, the President asked us to leave. He wanted a one-on-one discussion.

The meeting took almost two hours.

When the two came out of the room, onlookers and government officials gave a long round of applause as they shook hands.

It seemed a truce at least had been reached.

"He has a brilliant mind," the President said after the meeting.

"Sometimes we misunderstand these people. He has a passion for the poor and thinks government has neglected the Western Province," he said.

Following the meeting, there was a 'ceasefire' of sorts from the Bishop. He maintained his counsel until towards the 2011 elections.

******

We were now working very well with the Church.

Some individual priests would invite the President for mass at their parishes and the President obliged.

When Bishop Merdado Mazombwe was appointed the first Zambian Cardinal by Pope Benedict XVI, the President facilitated a number of prominent Catholics to accompany the bishop to his consecration at the St. Peter's Basilica in the Vatican. The former archbishop of Lusaka Adam Koziowiecki of polish origin was the first cardinal in Zambia.

When they returned, the President hosted a special luncheon, attended by senior Catholics, at State House in honor of the newly ordained.

He also organized assistance for a number of Catholic Church projects, especially those run by nuns.

The President was a permanent guest at St. Ignatius Parish in Lusaka at Easter to watch plays performed by children. His granddaughter, a strong catholic, was one of the regular participants.

Occasionally, the President would pay a courtesy call on his friend, Right Reverend James Spaita, who was the Archbishop of Kasama. The two would meet for several hours over a meal and discuss national issues.

But even though there was the appearance of a thaw the church still had issues with the authorities. These included governance, education and poverty eradication.

The church felt that the government was not addressing those issues adequately.

In due course, the Bishops met and agreed to issue a pastoral letter detailing their concerns.

The letter titled "*A Call for Integrity*" was issued in March 2010 and talked of an approaching crisis.

"We face many challenges of governance and survival, among which, are increasing poverty and the presence of abject poverty, a pervading cancer of corruption and spiraling job losses," it said.

It also described government efforts to reform the constitution as a waste of money and poor people would not benefit.

The letter was not well received by the government. Vice President George Kunda, himself a devout Catholic hit back expressing himself against the church's involvement in politics.

"...In the Catholic Church there are priests who have joined the tirade of insulting, even insulting me and insulting the President," he said.

He accused the Catholics of backing the opposition leader Michael Sata, a Catholic. He referred to one of Sata's campaign meetings where he urged Zambians to vote for a Catholic who would run the country on Catholic Church principles.

A freelance journalist, Chanda Chimba, who was allied to the ruling party, produced documentaries that depicted the Catholic Church as partisan supporting the opposition. The documentaries were quite hard-hitting on the Church and the Bishops.

"Dickson, try to moderate these programmes. Fighting the Catholic Church won't take us anywhere," one minister, who was a Catholic, told me.

Some party members also joined in the attacks, accusing the Catholics of all sorts of things, even referring to issues of homosexuality and child abuse that rocked the Church in the west.

The Church responded strongly in a pastoral letter titled "*Where there is hatred let me bring love*". It stated in part:

"In recent months, we have all witnessed a growing barrage of attacks in the public media against the Catholic Church in Zambia, its leadership, priests and even its doctrine," read the first part of the letter of May 19, 2011.

"When these attacks distort the Catholic Church's moral doctrine on celibacy or homosexuality, we all have cause for alarm," the statement read, delivered by the Right Reverend George Lungu, Bishop of Chipata who was President of the ZEC.

The letter was to be read in all Catholic churches in Zambia on ascension Sunday - June 5, 2011.

"Our engagement in politics is only motivated by our divine obligation to speak on behalf of the voiceless in our country. In exercising this prophetic ministry, we will be neutral in so far as partisan politics are concerned."

The letter attracted more verbal exchanges between government and the Church until a meeting was convened with the Bishops at State House. It was of the straight-talking type.

It was a packed high-level meeting that started with a prayer before going into the nitty-gritty.

I sat in the meeting as note-taker, although I contributed twice regarding the accusation against the public media.

"There are no instructions to the public media to attack the Catholic Church," I said.

Even though I was not Catholic myself, my children were baptized and were active members of our parish. We had also a number of ministers, including the national chairman of the governing party, Michael Mabenga, who were devout Catholics.

"Since all public media is owned and controlled by government, we can safely conclude that these attacks on our Church are sponsored by government. Whatever the case, this not the way of winning the Catholic vote in an election year," the Bishops responded, reciting lines from the pastoral letter.

"Why has the Church failed to discipline priests who are attacking the President every day?" the Vice President asked.

"Those views do not represent the views of the Church. The Church's position is expressed by ZEC," was the answer.

"When we speak, as Bishops, our message has nothing to do with any perceived dislike or preference for any particular sitting President or any political party. We therefore refuse to be intimidated, cowed into silence or to compromise or be silenced on national issues, important issues that affect the poor people," was their response, again taken from the pastoral letter.

The Vice President was hard on the church.

"Mr. Vice President, we wonder where you did your catechism," one Bishop asked amidst laughter.

The meeting ended with a pledge to continued dialogue and a closing prayer.

But that was not to be.

A few priests tried to pursue reconciliation by engaging the President and his office while others increased the barrage of attacks. The governing party and its members reciprocated, sometimes harshly.

The attacks from both sides continued until the election.

The opposition ruthlessly exploited the perceived wedge between the President and the Catholics and threw its weight behind the Catholics.

"The Catholic Church has been very fair, if the Catholic Church was anti-MMD, this government would have collapsed. The Catholic Church knows so many things that the MMD criminals have committed," Sata was quoted as saying in the March 9, 2010 *The Post* edition.

The privately-held media would show Sata, on his knees in a Catholic Church, praying with congregants.

On the other hand, non-Catholic churches backed the President and the ruling party. It created the impression that the President, who was Anglican, favored the charismatic churches. The perception was permeated by the fact that the Minister who called the Catholic Church 'genocidal' was an ordained preacher of the Pentecostal church.

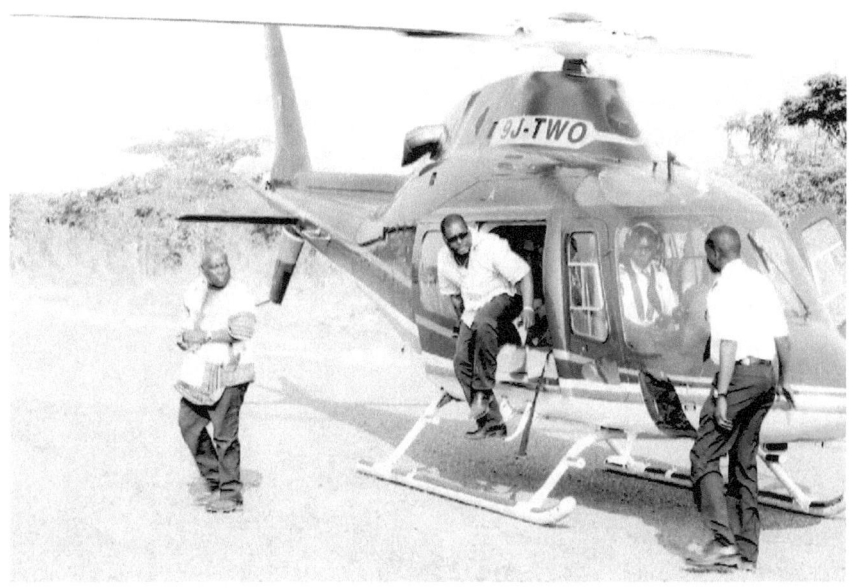

Alighting from the chopper in Nchelenge District,
Luapula during the 2011 Presidential elections © Post Newspaper

With President Banda during one of the campaign rallies in 2011

Having a drink with then main opposition leader late Anderson Kambela Mazoka in 2006

With then opposition leader Michael Sata at a polling station during the 2006 Presidential elections

With Robinson Nkonde, the President's senior private secretary & Dr. Shaileni Desai, the President's personal physician in 2010 in China

At the Great Wall of China in 2010 © Zanis

With Bob Samakai pose and Swaziland King Mswati during the 2009 Reed Dance in Swaziland.

Having a light moment with Swaziland king during the 2009 State visit to the kingdom of Swaziland as President Banda looks on

President Banda congratulates me after being sworn in as Special Assistant to the President in 2009.

Giving last minutes tips to President Banda before going live to address the nation when he dissolved parliament in 2011 © Zanis

Bidding farewell to Burundi president Pierre Nkurunzinza

Shaking hands with Chinese President Hu Jintao in China during the State Visit in 2010 © Zanis

Talking to journalists after being elected chairman of the Media Institute of Southern Africa (MISA) Zambia 2003

Being congratulated by scores of people outside the Lusaka High Court when I was acquitted of espionage charges in 2000 © Henry Salim

With President Banda at one of the spot interviews at the Lusaka International Airport

With Chief of Protocol Bob Samakai having a drink on one of the presidential trips on a Challenger Jet

President Banda weeps as he concedes defeat in presidential poll

Shaking hands with newly elected President Michael Sata in September 2011 at the handover ceremony © Henry Salim

Chatting with President Banda & legal advisor Joseph Jalasi at State House in 2009 shortly after we were sworn in as Special Assistants to the President

With President Banda at State House walking to a function to handover tractors to farmers © Markson Wasamunu

With South African jazz maestro Jonathan Butler in Lusaka during one of his visits

President Banda introducing me to then Egypian President Hosni Mubarak at the Presidential Palace in Cairo 2010

Being welcomed to Turkey by President Abdullah Gul in Ankara at the Presidential Palace in July 2010

With former Lusaka City mayor Fisho Mwale at the annual Ncwala Ceremony of the Ngoni people in Eastern Zambia in 2008

As Commissioner at one of the public sittings getting views on the country's new constitution in 2004.

Inside the Presidency

On one of the many foreign trips with the President

With President Jacob Zuma of South Africa and President Banda during a joing press conference in Lusaka. Next to President Zuma is his spokesman Vincent Mangwenya

With President Banda monitoring the November 2011 elections in the Democratic Republic of Congo under the Carter Centre.

At a news conference during the Lesotho elections with former Malawi president Bakili Muluzi and former Nigeria president Yakubu Gowon

Inside the Presidency

President Banda
at 'monkey' press
confence
(above)

The rogue monkey
(left)

*Pictures as captured
by Reuters*

DICKSON JERE JOKES WITH FORMER ZAMBIA'S PRESIDENT DR. FREDERICK CHILUBA (SECOND FROM RIGHT), HIS WIFE (SECOND FROM LEFT) AND EMMANUEL MWAMBA AT INTERCONTINENTAL HOTEL LUSAKA, ZAMBIA ON WEDNESDAY JULY 7, 2010. PICTURES BY SALIM HENRY/SHENPA. © 2010

My children Siyabonga, Khuzwayo & Mandhla

With friend James Banda

With Alderman Tom Mtine at the 2010 AfCON in Angola

With FAZ president Kalusha Bwalya and former national team coach Dario Bonetti

SPECIAL Assistant to the President for press and public relations Dickson Jere with Ivory Coast Prime Minister Guillaume Soro at a press briefing at Taj Pamodzi Hotel in Lusaka - Picture by JOHN NGOMA

PRESIDENT Banda's press aide, Dickson Jere (c) consults with South African President Jacob Zuma (r) during a joint press conference at State House December 8, 2009. To the left of President Banda. PHOTO/NOELMARKSON

With Joe Kaunda and Amos Malupenga

In Paris, France while working for AFP, 2000

With former republican president Dr. Kenneth David Kaunda

President Banda introducing me to Rwanda president Paul Kagame

With friend Verona Miyanda at my graduation   With former Minister Mike Mulongoti and Tenthani Banda

Munali Debate Panel: Standing: myself, Mweemba Kawala and Nalumino Nalumino Seated: Wellington Chota and Elton Mposha, former Lusaka Mayor

Former Presidents Chiluba and Kaunda at the Cathedral of the Holy Cross with President Banda.

Presidential aides Richard Chembe, myself, Dr. Austin Sichinga and Dr. Shaileni Desai relaxing in Instabul, Turkey

At my farm in Chipata, 2012

In Dubai, 2012

Addressing a conference of Chief Justices of Malawi in 2003

Acting Chief Justice Lombe Chibesakunda with High Court Judges seated and newly admitted lawyers

With my sponsor Bradford Machila at my call day on March14, 2014 at the Supreme Court

CHAPTER THIRTEEN
WORKING WITH A SPORTING PRESIDENT

It took a telephone call from President Rupiah Banda to the president of the world soccer governing body, the Federation of International Football Associations (FIFA), Stephen (Sepp) Blatter, to save Zambia's football from an international ban.

The Football Association of Zambia (FAZ) was ridden by internal divisions that resulted in two parallel executive committees - both claiming legitimacy.

FIFA was concerned and was ready to crack the whip if the confusion persisted. But there was no solution in sight, as the two 'warring' parties would not see eye to eye.

The President, a staunch and lifelong soccer fan, watched from a distance before intervening to the save the situation.

"*FIFA warns Zambia of consequences of dispute within FAZ,*" read a British Broadcasting Corporation (BBC) headline of the online edition of November 30, 2010.

"Get me the number for Blatter," the President told me after I showed him the report.

Apart from my regular job, he had assigned me the additional responsibility of looking after the interest of the country's national football team as well as other sports. Like him, I was a football fan.

I was appointed coordinator of fundraising for the team on behalf of the President. A committee was formed and bank account opened where companies deposited funds to support the team's preparations.

I thought handling football and sports issues would be a breather from the stress of the political arena but was to discover otherwise. There was a lot of intrigue and firefighting involved.

After a brief conversation with Blatter, the President looked relieved.

"He has agreed to meet the two camps and resolve the matter," the President who was the patron and lifelong member of the FAZ said.

He asked me to draft a follow-up letter to the FIFA president thanking him for his kind understanding and to also inform him of the delegation that was expected to travel to Zurich, Switzerland, for the meeting.

The delegation headed by the Sports minister Kenneth Chipungu included Zambia's football icon who was now president of the FAZ Kalusha Bwalya and the executive opposed to him was headed by businessman Andrew Kamanga

In total, six members were in the government delegation that also included the National Sports Council of Zambia (NSCZ), a statutory body established to run sports in the country.

FIFA refused to recognize the second executive led by Kamanga and threatened to ban Zambia from all football activity if the dispute was not resolved.

The Zurich meeting resolved that a joint meeting of the two contenders be held and a new executive be elected to run football in Zambia. It was a major breakthrough and the president's intervention cheered the fans.

"I am happy with the outcome," he said later on.

He had monitored the events in Zurich from the time the delegation arrived in the city.

Football in Zambia is popular and a unifying factor. The President had a track record in the game and was well known in football circles.

He played a major role in the development of football, boxing and other sports in the country.

He once served as vice-chairman of the FAZ and was the chairman of the first association of football fans called the 'Bola-bola Group'. When he was foreign affairs minister, he told me that the then President of Zambia, Kenneth Kaunda, allowed him to take days off his busy schedule to accompany the national football team on international engagements.

"We used to charter planes with a lot of supporters whenever the team played outside Zambia," he would remember with nostalgia.

The President was also chairman of the Chiparamba Soccer Academy, founded by his soccer-loving son, Nenani. It is this academy that contributed over five players to the National Team that in 2012 won the African Cup of Nations (AFCON) in Gabon. It was the first time that Zambia had won the cup!

As President, he gave football the highest attention.

He personally was involved in fundraising for the national team. He hosted meetings at State House for private companies that pledged support for the team. At that time, his dream was for Zambia to win the AFCON and qualify for the World Cup.

Inside the Presidency

"I am convinced this time around we are going to win the Africa cup and qualify for the World Cup," he would tell the meetings.

In one meeting, the Canadian mining giant, First Quantum Minerals took up the entire budget of the team and purchased vehicles for the technical staff following a meeting with the President.

Each time the team won a game, the President would call me asking if I had prepared a congratulatory message.

"Please issue a statement immediately to congratulate the boys," he would say.

A letter to the players followed my statements.

"I strongly believe this team can qualify for the World Cup if they remain focused in the remaining games," the President said in his statement of March 29, 2009 when Zambia held Egypt to a goalless draw in Cairo.

During the 2010 Africa Cup of Nations tournament in Angola, he flew to Luanda to meet the players at the start of the tournament.

There was a carnival atmosphere.

The President, clad in Zambian livery, sang and danced to boost morale among players when he met the team at the departure lounge of Quatro de Fevereiro International Airport in Luanda, Angola.

Prayers and Bible readings preceded the President's address to the players and technical staff.

"It is our time," the President told the players who were all smartly dressed in black suits.

He then shook hands and hugged each player before seeing them off to northern Angola where the team was based during the group stages.

The team performed well and reached the quarterfinals, which they lost to Nigeria 5 – 4 on post-match penalties following a goalless 120 minutes of regulation and extra time.

"The President observed that the Zambian team was very well coordinated and played superior football compared to their opponents," said the statement released shortly after the game.

He decided that the team deserved a hero's welcome home.

"I am sending my plane to pick the team up," he said.

I contacted the Zambia Air Force command and they immediately dispatched the presidential plane to Angola.

The team was very happy with that treatment.

Later, he hosted a special luncheon at State House where he congratulated them for the performance. "Where is the coach?" he asked after noticing that his 'son' was not at the luncheon.

He was told that the French coach Herve Renard had remained behind for some assignment.

Renard, who had taken charge of the national team, became like a son to the President. Through me, he had direct contact with the President.

"Please bring Renard for a cup of tea," the President would occasionally tell me.

"I want to find out if all is well with the team," he would say.

We used to meet Renard and his assistant Patrice Beaumelle at Nkwazi House where he discussed the team's condition and the challenges that faced the technical bench.

It was as a result of those interactions that I have remained a close friend to the coach.

******

Two weeks after the Africa cup tournament, the coach was nowhere to be seen and never came back thereafter.

He had been "poached" by Angola.

"Sorry Dickson, I have moved to Angola. Say bye to the boss," a text message from the coach reached me via my mobile.

I briefed the President who looked disturbed by the news.

"How could that happen?" he wondered before telling me to wish him well in his "future endeavors."

The Zambia football team was now without a coach.

Each time the national team was in camp, the President took time off his busy schedule to watch the boys in training. At times, he would invite sponsors to join him.

He did that religiously especially if he would miss the actual game.

The players loved the support. He would address them like a coach on the pitch before going away from the field.

******

"We want a coach. We want a coach, we want a...," scores of football fans chanted, mobbing the President as he left Nkoloma Stadium in Lusaka.

He had gone to watch the national team in training.

"Dickson, have you heard what they are saying?" he asked as he stopped to address them.

"I promise, I will look into that," he told the cheering fans.

When we got back to State House, he called me for a meeting.

"You heard for yourself, we need to do something about the issue of the coach," he said.

The following day, we held a meeting with the Ministry of Sports and Sports Council officials where the issue of a coach was tabled.

FAZ had no money to hire an expatriate coach.

"We have to find money," the President said.

He telephoned the Minister of Finance and asked him to consider putting a budget line for a football coach to assist FAZ. Football is a unifying sport in Zambia and could not be left to FAZ alone.

The process of looking for a new coach began.

Names were being suggested in the press as well as football circles.

During that period, the President travelled to attend the 2010 Africa-France summit in the French resort town of Nice. After the summit, he travelled to Monaco for scheduled meetings.

It was while having lunch with a European businessman and sports administrator that the name Dario Bonetti cropped up. Dario was a former Italian national team defender as well as a kingpin of the Italian Serie A teams: Roma, Milan and Juventus.

"He was interested in the job," one of his contacts told us.

Having looked at his CV, the President and other delegation members were impressed.

"Let's invite him to meet with the Sports Council and FAZ," the President said.

Dario and his crew of four assistants traveled to South Africa where he joined the President and his delegation at the 2010 World Cup tournament.

After the games, a meeting was held which was attended by the Minister of Sports Kenneth Chipungu, FAZ President Kalusha Bwalya and his general secretary and officials from the sports council. I, too, attended the two meetings held in Pretoria and Johannesburg.

That is how the Italian got the job.

On his first visit to Zambia, he came to State House.

The President and I were in a cabinet meeting when a note was passed to me that Dario was waiting to see me outside. I passed it to the President as I walked out.

"Dickson, this is important, let him come and meet the Ministers," the President said and told the cabinet ministers that Dario was the new national football team coach.

The following day, his engagement made the headlines on the sports pages.

One minister made everyone laugh when he quickly googled and discovered that the coach had the world record of having been suspended for a total 39 matches in 2009.

"Hope he will not bring that indiscipline to the team," he said amidst laughter.

Subsequent stories alleged that State House had directly employed the coach without the knowledge of FAZ or the Sports Council.

In consultation with the President, I issued a statement the following day and explained the two meetings in South Africa that resulted in his being hired.

Dario worked hard and qualified the national team to the 2012 Africa Cup of Nations in Gabon although he was sacked before the tournament. Renard was re-enagaged and drilled the team, which eventually won the cup.

But during his tenure as coach, the media thought he was too arrogant and only respected the views of State House and not even views of FAZ.

The President was accused of having "single-sourced" the coach.

He was sacked after the President lost the 2011 elections.

******

The relationship between FAZ and government was not always good. FAZ officials constantly accused the Minister of Sports and his team of interfering in the running of football.

The Ministry insisted that it had a role, especially considering that government was the major funder of the sport.

"We give FAZ money and should therefore have a say," Mr. Chipungu would insist.

When he tried to call for accountability, FAZ always rushed to FIFA, which came down very hard on the government, threatening suspension of Zambia from international football.

At one point, the government withheld funding to the national team, which had a scheduled game against Mozambique coming up.

"Please help resolve this issue," FAZ President Bwalya telephoned me after he reached a deadlock with government officials.

I immediately informed the President.

"We can't allow the boys to suffer because of a fight between FAZ and the Minister," he said.

Within minutes, he was on the phone to the Minister.

He directed that funds be released and that a government accountant travel with the money and handle all payments without the involvement of FAZ.

"FAZ exposes President Banda's lies on National Team" a headline on the *Zambian Watchdog* read, in a story which quoted officials as saying that the President had stopped payments to the team.

I had to do some damage limitation and issued a statement indicating that it was the President who authorized the release of funds following a direct request by FAZ to his office.

When FIFA officials visited Zambia, the President called a meeting with FAZ and the sports council to discuss the latest standoff with FIFA. FAZ and the sports ministry had differences over funds, mainly the welfare of foreign coaches and their salaries, which had not paid for a while.

"Why is it interference when government gives FAZ money?" the President asked.

He was concerned that FIFA only came in when government demanded accountability but was quiet when FAZ received assistance from the same governments.

It was a frank discussion.

The matter was resolved smoothly and quietly following the discussions.The President was in the news again over football. This time around the issue was to do with the World Cup trophy which was on a global tour. The FIFA delegation arrived in Zambia with the trophy, which was supposed to be presented to the President. He was not available for the occasion. He was accused of snubbing FIFA officials when they unveiled the trophy. *The Post* newspaper reported that FIFA was upset with the President's absence at the event, which was officiated by the Vice-President George Kunda.

The trophy was supposed to be touched by the President, the story said.

"We apologize to the Zambian government for this. We apologize to the President," the FIFA delegation leader Emmanuel Maradas told the media after he read the story.

He had telephoned me to respond to the story. Prior to the trophy event, I had informed the FIFA delegation that the President had prior engagements and would not make it to the presentation.

******

The President also wanted to develop sports facilities in Zambia. During his tenure, he laid the foundation stone for the construction of the new stadium in the second city of Ndola and subsequently christened the Levy Mwanawasa stadium. It was built and completed during his term of office.

He later organized a US$94 million concessional loan from the Peoples' Republic of China for the construction of stadia in Lusaka, which involved the redevelopment of the old Independence Stadium.

"The new stadia will be popular venues, hosting domestic and international football and other sporting events as well as social and cultural activities," the President said at the launch of the two projects on January 11, 2011.

His plan was for Zambia to host its first African Cup of Nations tournament during his tenure.

He was also involved in the development and promotion of other sports. He became a well-known boxing promoter through his stables, which he co-managed with his German Business partner Wilfrid Sauerland.

It was through his stables that the great Zambian boxer Lottie *Gunduzani* Mwale shot to stardom. Mwale was the first Zambian boxer to win the Commonwealth Light Heavyweight and African Boxing Union titles.

Twice as president, he hosted luncheons in honour of Zambia's female boxer, Esther Phiri, who was a double champion, holding the Women's International Boxing Association and World Boxing Organization titles. Other titles she held included those of the World Super Lightweight, Global Boxing Union and the Global Boxing Council.

The President also held two meetings with the International Judo Federation (IJF) President Marius Viser, which resulted in Zambia becoming the first African country to be given an IJF grant in the form of a Judo Centre.

I was asked to coordinate the programme although I had an interest in the matter as Vice President of the Zambia Judo Federation.

The President, in an unprecedented move, honoured two judokas with national medals. Roman Catholic priest, Father Jude McKenna was presented with the President's Insignia of Honour for his contribution to judo in Zambia while Gold Medalist

Shapa Wakung'uma was presented with the President's medal for meritorious achievement.

"It is because of Dickson Jere," one online article commented, saying I had influenced the President to recognize judo with such awards because I was a member of the executive. But this wasn't the case at all.

******

In his efforts to improve sports in Zambia, President Banda held high-level meetings with the International Olympic Committee (IOC) headed by its President at the time, Jacques Rogge.

He and Rogge jointly opened the ultramodern sports facility in Zambia called the Olympic Youth Development Centre (OYDC).

The President visited the IOC headquarters in Lausanne, Switzerland during one of his European engagements.

All these underlined the President's interest in sports and belief in its development.

At State House, he always kept footballs for donating to youth groups whenever he visited the countryside.

CHAPTER FOURTEEN
"A DAMN GOOD PRESIDENT"

It was March 15, 2005.

Police swung into action and seized over 100 pairs of shoes, 300 shirts and 150 suits from Zambia's second President Frederick Chiluba. The clothes were part of the former President's wardrobe, which comprised of high-heeled handmade shoes variously made from python, crocodile and ostrich skin, satin and lanvin suits and silk pajamas. The clothes were seized as part of an operation to recover goods that the former President was alleged to have acquired corruptly during his two - term tenure as president.

The seized personal effects, many still in their wrappings, were stored in a private warehouse. They were displayed to prove that the former President was greedy and corrupt and that he lived sumptuously while the majority of Zambians wallowed in poverty. The clothes were monogramed with his initials FJT for Frederick Jacob Titus.

"It is sad that the fight against corruption is being reduced to discussing suits, shirts, ties and shoes," Mr. Chiluba said in his angry reaction and said the government was trying to draw a comparison between him and the family of the former Philippines President Ferdinand Marcos whose wife Imelda left behind 1,200 pairs of shoes when the couple fled Manila in 1986.

"What they have done is to bring my underpants out to the general public," he said.

The government sued the former President and his associates in London for the recovery of money they were alleged to have stolen.

But the former President refused to appear before the London court of Judge Peter Smith, saying British courts had no jurisdiction to hear a crime committed in Zambia. After a protracted trial, Judge Smith on May 4, 2007 found Chiluba liable and was ordered to pay back to the Government of Zambia the sum of US$39 million.

"The people of Zambia will know that whenever FJT appears in public wearing a smart handmade suit or a pair of his 'signature' shoes they were acquired by stealing money from the public, the vast majority of whom live at subsistence levels," Judge Smith said in his judgment.

Chiluba hit back saying he was not going to respect the judgment.

"At best, this judgment is a mere political statement made by a man who represents a vicious and violent system with inherent prejudices and hatred against Africa," he said.

Smelling blood, civil society groups demanded that the judgment be registered in Zambia in order to recover the money from the former president.

The London judgment needed to be registered in Zambia for it to have legal effect.

The process of registering it was equally lengthy characterized by adjournments.

At the same time, government instituted criminal proceedings against Mr. Chiluba for theft of US$500,000, from an Intelligence Service account domiciled in London. It was an equally lengthy trial marred by technical adjournments and those caused by the former president's failing health and his need for medical treatment outside the country. In court, his lawyers argued among other things, that as former president, he could only be prosecuted for offences he committed in his personal capacity. Intelligence matters were government business, they argued. The trial went on for eight years!

When he became President in 2008, Mr. Rupiah Banda found these cases still in process. There was an expectation in some circles that he would push for the jailing of the former President as well as recover the money the London court found to have been stolen.

At that time, Chiluba's wife, Regina, had already been found guilty and sentenced to three and half years in jail for allegedly receiving stolen property from her husband. She obtained bail pending appeal.

"I am not the court, I am only the President," the President said in view of the public debate.

He also reminded Zambians that Chiluba had in 1993 locked him up and several other opposition politicians on a trumped up charges of plotting a coup that came to be known as the "Zero Option". It was alleged that the opposition politicians including the President, then a member of the United National Independence Party (UNIP) led by Dr. Kaunda, were plotting to topple the government.

"I should be the one holding a grudge against him but he was a President and I think a damn good President," Banda said when asked about his close links to the corruption-tainted former President.

The President and Chiluba didn't have close relations *per se*, although the latter supported him in the 2008 presidential elections. After those elections, the former President made himself available to assist the new President in developing party programmes as the founding leader. The President also extended invitations to the former President to attend state functions and were occasionally seen seated together.

It was strongly believed, by the opposition and civil society groups, that the President and his new political ally were in a deal to let Chiluba off the hook over the alleged crimes he committed.

"*Rupiah, Chiluba possess Dubious Character,*" was the headline in *The Post* edition of July 27, 2009. The story quoted the opposition leader Michael Sata.

"Chiluba and him (Banda) are birds of the same feather," Sata said, referring to corruption.

When the court acquitted Chiluba of the US$500,000 theft charge on August 17, 2009, a slew of accusations followed. The President was accused by the opposition and civil society groups of having interfered with the case in order to secure the acquittal of his political ally.

"He even congratulated Chiluba when judgment was still being read in court. How did he know that Chiluba would be cleared?" *The Post* editorial asked.

In fact on the day that the former President was acquitted, I had traveled with the President to Kabwe, a mining town about 100 kilometers north of Lusaka. He was the guest speaker at the annual conference of the Council of Churches in Zambia.

When we arrived at the conference the President called me.

"Keep me informed of whatever verdict comes from the court. I want to know," he said and he instructed me to pass the message on to the podium if he would still be delivering his speech.

"It is very important," he said.

He had whispered to me and colleagues that if the former President was found guilty, he would turn his home into a prison for him to be under house arrest because of Chiluba's deteriorating health. He had an acute heart condition.

My colleague, Joseph Jalasi, the legal advisor remained in Lusaka to follow the court proceedings. He had strict instructions to deliver the news to me immediately judgment was pronounced.

My telephone beeped just before lunchtime. It was a text message from Jalasi saying the former President had been acquitted.

I drafted a small note and walked up to the podium in the packed hall. I slipped it on top of the President's speech, bowed and walked back. Before I could reach my chair, the President deviated from the written speech.

"My young colleague has just informed me that the former President has been acquitted," he said to the conference. Some delegates clapped.

"I feel relieved..." the President said, before he congratulated Chiluba for having won the case.

This statement would later be twisted by his political opponents. They alleged that he spoke before judgment was delivered. It was not true. Next, they alleged that the judgment was not fair and asked the President to instruct the prosecutors to appeal.

"I am not the Director of Public Prosecutions (DPP)," the President responded and it is the case that the constitution of Zambia gives powers of appeal only to the DPP.

"The devil has tried to put the stigma of a thief on me, but God has dealt with the devil," the former President said following his acquittal.

Soon a sustained campaign against the President was launched by different groups saying his refusal to appeal the judgment was a clear indication that he had interfered with the case. Unknown to the DPP, the private prosecutors who handled the case appealed to the high court. They were instructed to do so by Max Nkole, who was head of the special *ad hoc* taskforce appointed by government to lead the prosecution of the former President and his associates, mainly senior members of his administration.

The DPP, Chalwe Mchenga, withdrew the appeal, leading to fresh accusations that he was working to the President Banda's orders.

******

Heated debate followed, during which the government decided to disband the special taskforce on corruption and fuse its operations into the Anti-Corruption Commission (ACC). The task force chairman Nkole, whose contract had expired, had to leave his position, prompting further accusations that he was being punished for having appealed against the verdict.

The government argued that it was spending too much money paying legal fees to private lawyers who handled the corruption cases when the Attorney General's chambers had qualified lawyers. Zambia for instance spent US$14 million in legal fees in the London case of the former President while US$720,000 was spent annually on local lawyers.

It was decided by Cabinet that the amounts were too large to be spent on an *ad hoc* institution instead of using it to build capacity within existing institutions.

"This decision was motivated and meant to stop people from talking about the acquittal of Chiluba," said Rueben Lifuka, President of Transparency International Zambia (TIZ).

The western aid donors joined in the debate, urging the government to show commitment to the fight against corruption or lose financial support. This riled the President.

"This is not a banana republic, it doesn't belong to anybody," he told reporters.

"Of course we are fighting against corruption. Why should just one case become a major one?' he asked before asking those meddling in internal affairs of the country to pack and go.

The taskforce was established by the President's predecessor Levy Mwanawasa who thought the ACC did not have adequate expertise to deal with high-level and sophisticated corruption.

The New York Times carried a detailed feature on June 10, 2009 titled "Battle to Halt Graft Scourge in Africa Ebbs" where it mentioned Zambia as a country where there was less commitment to tackling corruption since President Banda came to power in 2008.

"The tempo, the intensity to tackle corruption is dropping," the article quoted Nkole as saying. Several other international media outlets put out similar views on Zambia, which put my office on the spot.

Several cases of corruption within government were being reported in the press at an unprecedented pace in order to show that the President was too lenient. Some aid donors withheld their support citing rising corruption.

******

The President had to personally deal with those concerns, I thought. I talked with him and he agreed to address the issues at a news conference.

"In the last eight months, a number of alleged corruption cases have been exposed," the President began and acknowledged the problem.

"Despite the erroneous and deliberate impression that has been created that corruption has escalated during my Presidency, it is clear that these cases predate my assumption of office," he said.

He explained that he believed in strengthening institutions and enacting new laws to curb corruption as opposed to merely arresting and charging people.

At that press conference, he announced the establishment of the Serious Frauds Unit within the Anti-Corruption Commission, the Financial Intelligence Unit at the Central Bank to monitor money movements. He ordered the Auditor General to carry out forensic audits on systems and procurement in major spending ministries and agencies.

He also introduced the Public Interest Disclosure Act for the protection of whistleblowers and the Forfeiture of Proceeds of Crime Act, which was aimed at confiscating assets acquired from stolen funds.

"I expect the new measures I have announced will strengthen the institutions involved in the fight against corruption," he concluded.

The speech was generally well received by most Zambians. However, the question of the former President's alleged corruption was not going away.

"Good speech by President but he has not said anything on the money Chiluba stole," read an email I received from a journalist shortly after the briefing.

We put out a dedicated spin on the 'President is soft on corruption' allegation and tried to show that he was working to curb the vice. Interviews were organized with both local and international media where the President and ministers responded to the concerns raised on the fight against corruption. Some documentaries were also produced that showed efforts by government to fight graft.

But baseline studies from different NGOs still showed that the President's actions were not enough. Zambians wanted to see more open actions such as the dismissal of ministers and permanent secretaries fingered in corrupt deals.

"The people want to see the implicated senior officials arrested and taken to court," read one of the reports compiled by a local NGO.

******

In trying to align the new changes to the law, government decided to remove a clause that criminalized 'abuse of office' by government officials and civil servants. The rationale presented by Vice President and Justice Minister George Kunda was convincing and cabinet accepted it. The 'abuse of office' law was killing the spirit of entrepreneurship among civil servants who were required to account for any asset they acquired while in office when the same was not demanded in the private sector. The clause also presumed the victims guilty until they proved themselves innocent by showing how they acquired the assets. It was considered unconstitutional.

But the move backfired on government.

"We the leaders of this country when we amass wealth, why don't we want people to question us about our wealth?" asked George Mpombo, the one-time defence minister who opposed the changes in parliament.

The bill went through after a heated debate and voting in the National Assembly. Still, the impression persisted that government leaders changed the law because they were stealing public funds and didn't want to be accountable after leaving office.

"This provision of the law has been key in securing corruption-related convictions in the last ten years," said the Law Association of Zambia, the statutory body of lawyers. It opposed the removal of the clause.

"Rupiah is preparing to plunder national resources by removing that law," Sata said.

In the midst of the debate, the President was invited to be the special guest at the centenary celebrations of the Anglican Church in Zambia at the Cathedral of the Holy Cross.

He was accompanied to the event by the former President Chiluba and other leaders. In the packed Church, the Anglican Bishop surprised everybody by launching an attack on the President and government for having removed the 'abuse of office law.'

"The fight against corruption should not be compromised and neither should we relent," the Bishop said as the congregation applauded while other congregants looked at the former President.

It was an embarrassing moment for the President.

The former President made some gestures, shaking his head in disapproval while constantly looking up the ceiling.

Another Bishop took to the pew and amplified on the issue.

"Your Excellency, when we speak as a Church, we are not against government. We speak for the people just as God commanded us," said Bishop Albert Chama.

I walked to the other clergy seated in the Church and whispered to them to control the messages before the event was spoilt by politics. By the time the President was delivering his speech, the atmosphere was tense.

After the Church service, the Anglican Church, where the President worshipped, apologized to him over the incident. The apology was followed by a letter weeks later.

At that time, it was slowly dawning on some of us that the former President was a liability to the President's image. But it was too late to make any meaningful decisions to change the situation.

"*Lazo* (Chiluba) is not helping win votes here," said one senior party official from the Copperbelt where the former President was perceived to be popular.

An internal opinion poll carried out by our consultants showed that the former President was not helping matters on the fight against corruption. The link to him was taking away the credit from the President's new anti-corruption measures.

The attacks on the President on corruption intensified when former intelligence chief, Xavier Chungu, who fled the country in 2004 after being arrested for corruption, returned to Zambia. He was a co-accused of former President Chiluba. On arrival he was arrested and taken to jail but the perception created was that he was invited back by the President.

"He has come back because he knows President Banda is tolerant to corruption," civil society groups said.

To make matters worse, Chungu issued a statement endorsing the President as the right man for the top job and urged Zambians to elect him.

"Let it be known that I am busy and in my own style campaigning for the President, Mr. Banda," said Chungu who was accused of high-level corruption committed when he was the spymaster.

That statement stirred a lot of criticism in the country although it was never authorized by anyone of us. It was his right to choose his candidate.

"Chungu's campaign for President Banda is just a way of saying thank you to the President," said Given Lubinda, an opposition lawmaker who was also chairperson of the African Parliamentarians against Corruption (APNAC).

******

The campaign team was trying to assess the role which the former President would play in the coming elections. The team wanted to use him in areas where he was going to be effective without bringing in the baggage of corruption to the campaign. His home area of Luapula province was identified as a possible place to deploy him.

I received a call from the former President.

"Hi Dick, I just wanted to say hello," he said in his usual jovial way before he cut the line.

I was surprised. Whenever he phoned it used to be a long conversation.

He dialed my number again.

"How is His Excellency?" he asked.

I told him the President was well although he had a family bereavement.

He said he wanted to see the President to personally pass his condolences.

I arranged for the meeting that same day. He later called me to say 'thank you' for arranging the meeting.

"By the way, if you have anything confidential from His Excellency, please give the message to my daughter Malama. I trust her a lot," he said, referring to his stepdaughter.

The following day on June 18, 2011, I accompanied the President to his home village where he attended the funeral of a family member.

While in Chipata, I received a telephone call from the Chief of Protocol Bob Samakai who had remained behind on that trip.

"Dr. Chiluba is dead," he said.

"Inform the Principal," Samakai said, his voice sounding hoarse.

He had received the news from the former President's personal physician. The former President died at his Kabulonga home after suffering a heart attack. He was 68.

The President was asleep by the time I got the message. I consulted with colleagues and it was decided not to disturb him. He had spent almost the whole day in the village at the burial of his relative. He was tired and needed to rest.

By early morning, the President got the news. It was devastating! He broke-down in disbelief. Tears rolled from his eyes continuously as I sat with him in his hotel room.

"You have to address the nation and officially announce the death," I said, as I handed him a copy of the speech I had prepared for the address.

"No, you do it yourself," the President refused. His body was shaking.

After further persuasion, he agreed.

I set up the studio in the gardens. The television crew was ready to shoot.

The President came out of the room, casually dressed. I was not going to pick a fight with him in that sorrowful mood over the dress code. Other aides tried to talk to him to wear a suit. He just brushed them aside.

"It is with deep sorrow and sadness that I formally announce the passing away of our dear former President Chiluba who died in the early hours of this morning," the President said.

"I appeal to the nation to mourn the late President with dignity and respect," he concluded his one-page speech.

A period of seven days of national mourning was declared and flags flew at half-mast during that time. The President wanted Chiluba to be given a state funeral befitting a former head of state with full military honors for the former Commander-In-Chief.

The obituaries that ran in the international press linked the President to the acquittal of the former President on the theft charge.

In the June 19, 2011 edition of *The New York Times*, the obituary stated that the President "has since disbanded much of the nation's anticorruption apparatus."

"Mr. Banda has referred to Mr. Chiluba as a *'damn good President'* and credited him with bringing political freedoms to the country," the report said.

It appeared that, even in death, the former President's tainted image stuck to the President!

CHAPTER FIFTEEN
A PRESIDENT FOR ALL ZAMBIANS!

In ecstasy members of the governing Movement for Multi-party Democracy (MMD) draped in the navy blue and white party colours waved replicas of the Zambian flag and portraits of the President. There was a song and dance atmosphere, and great excitement as the President arrived for the MMD national convention.

It was April 5, 2011 and the venue: Mulungushi Rock of Authority, outside the Central province capital of Kabwe about 100 kilometers north of Lusaka. It was a historic setting. Mulungushi was the venue of some of the most significant anti-colonial political meetings that led to the country's independence on October 24, 1964.

The atmosphere was tumultuous and at times chaotic as the party faithful surged forward to touch or greet the President. A security cordon soon formed around him to ensure that he reached the podium unimpeded.

The President was in party colours too with a strapline at the back of his shirt that read: *"A President for all Zambians"* – his campaign slogan. It was to become something of his trademark as the campaign wore on.

He walked arm in arm with his wife on the red carpet as he entered the arena.

I walked behind him with other State House aides as he waved to the cheering crowd, making impromptu stops to shake hands. This was the second extraordinary MMD National Convention called to elect the MMD Presidential candidate in the General Election scheduled for later that year. The convention would also elect members of the party National Executive Committee, NEC.

Diplomats, civil society groups and representatives of the governing political parties in the Southern African region sat watching the endless dances and listened to solidarity songs. First President, Kenneth Kaunda and second President Frederick Chiluba were in attendance.

When the President reached the podium he did a jig, which sent the crowd into a new frenzy.

"The hour!" he chanted the party slogan.

"Has come!" the cheering crowd responded before the meeting was called to order.

For the first time in months, the party looked united. Members danced together and there were no visible signs of the infighting that had rocked it in recent months.

The organization of the convention was perfect.

I felt good, as I was one of those tasked by the President to work with the party organizers to put together that convention that brought together over 3,000 delegates from across the country.

I shuttled between my office at State House and Mulungushi, the venue of the convention, just to make sure everything was in order.

"I want the convention to be well organized. Let our members enjoy.... I want plenty of music," the President had told me..

Almost all leading musicians in the country were there, competing with their tunes in praise of the President.

On the lawn of the conference venue, several spits of lamb, goat and sheep were roasting and there was a cloud of smoke.

"We have been well looked after," one delegate said to the President during a vote of thanks.

The tempo was high.

******

We had picked intelligence that some disgruntled party members wanted to obtain a court injunction to stop the President from standing for election on grounds that he was ineligible. We kept our fingers crossed.

The party wanted a leader who would be constitutionally eligible to contest the forthcoming presidential election. Detractors spread the story that he was born of a Zimbabwean father and a Malawian mother, making him ineligible to run as President of Zambia.

"Why is this issue coming up now? The President contested and won the last elections without anyone accusing him of being a foreigner," I told the press when they sought a comment.

"The President has never hidden his background. He was born in Zimbabwe to Zambian parents," I said.

His lawyers were on standby in Lusaka in case the attempt materialized

At the close of nominations, the President was unopposed.

"I, therefore, declare Banda Rupiah Bwezani duly elected President of the MMD for the next five years," the returning officer pronounced amidst applause.

He was now the official presidential candidate for the governing party.

State House aides were among the first to congratulate 'the boss'. It looked like the Banda juggernaut was set for a crushing victory at the general elections later in the year.

Most of the President's key ministers went through unopposed in elections to the national executive committee of the party. Some opponents withdrew from the race following late night political horse-trading. The President worked for smooth elections and unity. I was at the centre of talks with some candidates. I shuttled among different camps to deliver the President's position.

He had for instance asked me to talk to candidates from Eastern province to withdraw from the race for key party positions to allow other regions to take them up since he was from that province.

"I am from Eastern province. I want a national chairman and national secretary from other regions. We need to balance power," he said.

The suggestion was not always well-received but nevertheless many complied.

The President preferred Vice President George Kunda to be the party Vice-President as well but faced massive opposition. Despite our entreaties, opposition to his candidature persisted. After consultations, the party decided to freeze the position of Vice President so that there was no election to the post. It became a face-saver for Kunda.

The convention also expelled wayward members of the party who were facing disciplinary charges. They included former ministers George Mpombo, Mike Mulongoti and Jonas Shakafuswa. The action was meant to emphasize the need for discipline in the party ahead of the elections

After three days of deliberations, the Convention concluded with a resolution of unity in the party.

"Let the spirit of oneness, the spirit of unity demonstrated at this Convention, be carried forward through the period of the campaign. With this spirit, we will surely win," the President told the meeting.

"The party must be geared and ready to campaign and win the coming elections. This is your number one task," he said in the closing address, which was also his acceptance speech.

When the opposition got the news that Mr. Rupiah Banda would be the standard-bearer for the governing party in the forthcoming elections, they applied for a court injunction to bar him from the race. They argued as we had heard earlier that he was not Zambian and was therefore ineligible. The biggest opposition party Patriotic Front (PF) filed a court action in the Lusaka High Court challenging the President's nationality. PF secretary general Wynter Kabimba also wanted the court to rule that the President committed perjury during the last election in 2008 when he swore an affidavit stating that his parents were Zambians by birth.

The President was livid when he was told of the court process. It was one of the few incidents that made him lose his cool.

"I don't like this kind of politics. Why are they bringing my late parents into politics?" he asked.

The high court judge Jane Kabuka, after hearings, threw out the challenge which cleared the way for President Banda to contest the elections.

MMD had earlier on wanted parliament to amend the constitution and introduce a clause that would requirea presidential candidate to be a holder of a university degree. This was targeted at PF leader Michael Sata who had no degree. Some opposition parties backed the proposal. Therefore, the nationality issue was seen as revenge by the PF.

"I am not interested in such things... let him stand. Zambians will decide whether they want an educated person or not," the President had said and the proposal was dropped.

******

After the convention, the President was back to his normal busy schedule. The party brass had wanted him to hit the campaign trail immediately after the convention, but his national duties could not allow it.

A feud developed between the President's aides and the party. We were accused of neglecting party issues by keeping the President busy with government-related duties at the expense of campaigning.

"You are enjoying in State House when it is the party which put the President in power," party officials would bluntly tell us.

Even though the party wanted the President to begin campaigning early, the official campaign period had not opened and the election date was still not set. Only the President could name the polling day.

We had agreed to reserve the President's energy for the official campaign. We knew the actual campaign was going to be tough and punishing. The official campaign usually takes five weeks and we had planned to keep the President on the move every day for that period.

"We need to reserve the President for those five weeks," one of the political consultants had advised.

After failing to convince State House to allow the President to start his campaigns early, some party members and senior civil servants bypassed us and started the process. They formed the President's campaign team and established a Campaign Centre.

One morning the President summoned me to his office.

He had received reports on the campaign team and Centre.

Do you know anything about this campaign centre?" he asked me.

I told him I was not aware of its existence.

"Please find out. I want you to go and check what's happening there," he said.

He instructed me to go with his political advisor Francis Chigunta. The President wanted a full report on the activities of the campaign team and the centre.

"I hear they are even raising funds in my name without authority," he said.

I quickly made telephone calls to get the details of the location before driving to the campaign centre. A few minutes after I left the office, I received a telephone call from the President.

"Please call me when you get to the place. I need to know what's going on there," he emphasized before hanging up.

I realized that there must be something amiss for the President to be that concerned.

The President's political advisor was in tow as we drove to the campaign center situated in the upmarket suburb of Kalundu. When we got there, we inspected the place, talked to staff before returning the call to the President. Former President Frederick Chiluba's son, we were told, owned the building.

"We are at the place..." before I could finish the sentence, the President cut in and advised us to urgently return to the office.

At the office, we found him with other senior State House aides and the Secretary to the Cabinet. He had more details on the centre and the names of people who were behind it. Two were senior civil servants in his government.

"I want a clean campaign. I don't want civil servants to be using office hours for campaigns," he told the meeting.

He instructed that whoever wanted to be part of the campaign team should first resign as a civil servant. He extended the ban to civil servants who had applied to stand as Members of Parliament. They must resign from the service.

"I don't want to have a civil service which is polluted with politicians," he said.

He turned to his political advisor and me:

"I have dissolved that campaign team and closed the centre," he said.

I chipped in, alerting him to the possible political repercussions if the campaign centre was to be housed at premises linked to the former President who was under severe attack for alleged corrupt practices.

He agreed.

"How can they start campaigning for me without my knowledge? I want an organized campaign team," he said.

"In 2008 elections, I lost a lot of money through uncoordinated activities. I want to plan it properly this year. I want it to be methodical," he said.

Veteran politician Vernon Johnson Mwaanga, alias VJ, a boyhood friend of the President headed the unauthorized campaign Centre. Mwaanga had been involved in almost all the presidential elections from 1991, which were won by the governing party. He was a self-styled strategist and electioneer who was known to deliver victories. But he had also earned the bad reputation of being an poll-rigger.

"I am removing VJ. He is not my campaign manager," the President said.

The dismissal of Mwaanga did not go well within the party. They accused us at State House of orchestrating the purge. We got verbal insults from party members who thought VJ was the only man who could deliver elections for the party and the President. He had a good command of supporters within the party.

The President later told reporters that he removed his friend because of the latter's 'questionable character'.

In Mwaanga's place, Deputy Minister Boniface Kawimbe was apponted to coordinate the President's campaign.

But the story that came out of the dismissal was something else.

It was alleged that Mwaanga had been sacked at the instigation of State House aides who were not happy with his closeness to the President.

"But as senior staff at State House, we don't mind what has happened to VJ because it is a relief. VJ's close relationship with the President was beginning to undermine our jobs as the President was listening more to what he was telling him," *The Post* newspaper of April 27, 2011 quoted an unnamed aide as saying.

I am not sure that the story headlined *"Rupiah drops VJ"* was really based on an interview with a presidential aide because we enjoyed good relations with Mwaanga. The President did reinstate him to his campaign team although with no particular responsibility.

By then the differences between officials in the party and State House had widened.

This prompted the President to attempt mending bridges between the party and his staff.

But the lower organs of the party continued to give us problems. They wanted unfettered access to the President which was not possible. So they decided to complain to the secretariat.

"We need to keep State House staff away from the President during party functions," was a resolution passed by some senior party officials.

At the launch of the 2011 MMD campaign, the party took over and showed us where real authority lay. We were made to stand at the back of the hall very far away from the President.

"You are making the President unpopular," was the accusation.

But they faced a problem. The President could not leave State House without our involvement.

At times the party would send a programme to the President to attend a meeting only to be told that he had another engagement that very day.

The party national secretary, Major Richard Kachingwe, took the initiative and called a meeting of presidential aides and the party.

"Let us cooperate. We are all working for the same cause," he told the meeting.

A new chapter of cooperation was established. We called each other 'cooperating partners' as we embarked on plans for the official campaign.

The President later named his full campaign team.

It was headed by Kawimbe, assisted by Dr. Martin Mtonga while his son, Henry, was the kingpin. The campaign team comprised of new faces while the old guards were relegated to some obscure responsibilities. A new campaign centre was opened and many young people volunteered for the poll challenge.

"I want everything to be coordinated by my team," the President said.

He emphasized the need for coordinated campaign messages as well as proper branding of the campaign, starting with vehicles, caps, T-shirts and so on. Everyone had to comply with the standards set by the team.

The Bell Pottinger team was helping with the designs and the materials as well as messaging. The pitch *"A President for All Zambians"* was put on every campaign material. The President was selling himself as someone who would look after every part of the country regardless of the party the area voted for.

I played a minimal role at the campaign centre although I was a contact for the consultants. We had known each other well from the 2008 elections and the President insisted that I work with them.

Everyone was preparing for the launch of the official campaign and the elections. At that time, we knew it was going to be a neck-to-neck battle between the President and his rival Sata. Our internal opinion poll had showed the closeness throughout that year. It promised to be a battle of the Titans.

CHAPTER SIXTEEN
CRYING WOLF AHEAD OF VOTING

Riot Police fired teargas to disperse angry protesters at Nakonde on the Zambia-Tanzania border. The unruly opposition supporters ran amok after they were .tipped. that a truck carrying pre-marked ballot papers for the forthcoming General election was about to cross the border.

Police had a tough time controlling the volatile situation.

The slogan-chanting youth wanted to set the truck ablaze.

"No rigging! No rigging! No rigging!" They shouted.

But the truck was carrying only boundary tape for marking polling station perimeters. Opposition supporters were, however, sure that it was carrying ballot papers pre-marked for the President.

Under police escort, the truck was driven to the police station in the border town where a public inspection of its cargo was conducted. The containers were opened in full view of the representatives of the opposition as well as independent NGOs.

******

Tension was high in other border towns as well.

Opposition supporters searched 'suspicious' trucks entering Zambia to make sure that there were no pre-marked ballot papers for rigging the elections.

The situation was worsened by loose talk by opposition leaders in Lusaka who insisted that the President and the Electoral Commission of Zambia (ECZ) were planning to steal the vote.

"Our members are on full alert to stop any attempt to rig the elections," said Given Lubinda, spokesman of the PF.

The President set September 20, 2011 as polling day in the general election and dissolved the national assembly, which signaled the beginning of the official campaign period.

The rigging accusations had started earlier that year following internal squabbles within the ECZ that led to the resignation of its chairperson Justice Florence Mumba. She stepped down on January 27, 2011 following noisy demands by her staff that she should leave or else they would not resume work. They accused her of malpractices over the procurement of audit services which the commission required. She had also sacked the director Dan Kalale who was widely believed in opposition circles to be the rigging mastermind.

But the opposition now claimed that she was hounded out on instructions from the government because she refused to accept rigging instructions and wanted to clean up the institution.

"The ECZ debacle is being orchestrated by your government for its ultimate benefit in this year's elections," Sata said in a letter to the President, which was released to the press.

The private daily, *The Post* newspaper, joined in defending the embattled chairperson saying she was being victimized because she wanted to put in place transparent systems at the ECZ ahead of the elections.

"Her efforts to clean up have galvanized significant resistance that is being openly supported by the government," its editorial of January 28, 2011 claimed.

The President replied terming the allegations "not only ridiculous but preposterous."

"My government has absolutely no hand at what has been going on at the ECZ," he said in a letter to Sata.

He reluctantly accepted the resignation of Judge Mumba and immediately replaced her with deputy chief justice Ireen Mambilima. She was an experienced election administrator having previously served as the ECZ chairperson before going back to the bench. She had presided over the 2006 elections before she left the commission to become the country's first female Deputy Chief Justice.

Parliament unanimously ratified her appointment as the ECZ chief and she immediately went full throttle to organize the elections.

The voter registration was the first assignment, which went smoothly despite a few logistical glitches. A total of 5,167,154 voters were on the updated roll out of a population of more than 13 million.

The second hurdle was the printing of ballot papers, which became a hot potato.

Zambia had no capacity to print them due to security and logistical limitations. The biggest printer, owned by the government, had no security printing facilities to undertake such a mammoth task.

The ECZ decided to print in South Africa with a company called the Universal Print Group (UPG).

The opposition disagreed.

They demanded the cancellation of the contract so that the ballots could be printed in Zambia. The South African company was also accused of corrupting some ECZ officials during the tendering process.

"Every political party and election observers will be present during the printing of the ballot papers in South Africa," Justice Mambilima assured.

But the tension continued to rise around the issue.

The First President of Zambia Kenneth Kaunda, whose children had declared for the opposition, joined the debate. He issued a strongly worded statement to the ECZ.

"The revelation that the printing company selected to print ballot papers has been involved in acts of corruption with ECZ officers is a grave indictment on the electoral process," Kaunda said.

"It breeds justifiable suspicion of possible collusion and electoral malpractices that may lead to the election results not being accepted by both the losers and the winners," he said.

The statement came as a shock to the government.

Kaunda was very close to the President and he often visited State House. The ECZ had also appointed him as 'peace ambassador' for the elections. He was expected to raise concerns with the ECZ quietly as he was part of the 'advisory team'.

This act called for damage control on our part.

I contacted his office to verify the statement. His aides denied any knowledge of it.

"He has been unwell and didn't even report for work. If that statement was from the old man, we would have known," the aide said.

We later discovered that some individuals allied to the opposition had taken an already prepared statement for him to sign at his house where he was on bed rest.

"These people are evil, how can they push an old man to issue such a statement," the President said when he was briefed. Meanwhile, *The Post* newspaper conducted a sustained media campaign against the printing of the ballot papers in South Africa and accused the President of having a hidden agenda.

"If we have post-election violence in this country, the ECZ will have to take full responsibility because there are things they can do to prevent the results that will be announced being rejected," the newspaper said, September 14, 2011.

The printing of the ballot papers, however, went ahead despite objections from the opposition. Civil society groups, churches and election monitors were flown to South Africa by the ECZ to observe the printing.

Despite accusations of planning to rig the elections, the President wanted free and fair elections. He was consistent on that point throughout his tenure. He was concerned that when the opposition won elections, there was no rigging but when the governing party won, there was an abundance of accusations.

Prior to the general elections, the opposition had won two key parliamentary by-elections with ballot papers printed by the same printer.

"We do not want this election to be marred by any irregularities. I remind all Zambians that election observers will be invited, that the eyes of the world will be upon us," the President said in his July 28, 2011 national address when he dissolved parliament and set the election date.

"Zambia has no need for lies, smears, political thuggery and negative campaigning. So I urge all candidates to adhere to the electoral code of conduct," he said.

Within the governing party, there were concerns that the President was too transparent in dealing with the opposition and the electoral process in general. Some members for instance raised eyebrows when he engaged some western diplomats on the electoral process. He held meetings with them regularly and told them to be free to familiarize themselves with the process of organizing the election.

"The boss is just too open to these people," one party official told me.

A debate had raged over the use of Parallel Vote Tabulation (PVT), a system of monitoring elections based on a representative sample of polling stations for independent verification of the official results.

The western donor countries and NGOs in Zambia supported the method while the ECZ, government and the governing party opposed it. There was no law in Zambia that allowed such a system.

"PVT is a stranger to us, its alien. We have never had it before," the President said when asked by reporters.

But the aid donors pushed for the system saying it was an effective way of validating the official results while the governing party thought it was an opposition ploy to transmit fake results.

The President asked me to organize a meeting with the proponents of PVT to discuss the issue in detail because there was too much speculation.

"I want to make an informed decision," he said.

"Nobody has convinced me on how the PVT will be used," he said.

I arranged a meeting for the President with representatives of the US-based National Democratic Institute (NDI), who were in the country to train NGOs on election monitoring. The President wanted to understand the process.

"This system has been used in various countries," said Professor Keith Jennings, the NDI delegation leader in Zambia.

I had worked with Professor Jennings in the 1996 presidential and parliamentary elections when he conducted elections monitoring training for political party agents and NGOs.

When I told the President I knew Professor Jennings, he decided to have the discussion over dinner with the NDI delegation at the Eviva Restaurant in Lusaka's Rhodespark suburb.

After hours of discussion, he was convinced that the system was not what he thought. But the argument still remained that there was no law that supported the use of such a method in Zambia.

"Tell the President to stop listening too much to these foreign organizations," another MMD member told me.

A strong perception was developing that western countries, especially the US, wanted the President out of power because they considered him to have failed to tackle corruption. There was no tangible evidence but the speculation continued. Such speculation is the daily menu for a President especially during elections.

The President largely ignored it.

When US Secretary of State Hilary Clinton visited Zambia, she asked the President for permission to meet the opposition leaders. She was on an official visit to Zambia and was hosted by the President, with dinner at State House and a joint press conference on the sidelines of the Africa Growth and Opportunity Act (AGOA) Forum which was held in Zambia that year.

"Why not?" was his answer after the Ministry of Foreign Affairs brought the request to his attention.

He even joked that she was going to discover the difference between himself and the contenders in terms of knowledge and decorum.

Some senior ruling party officials were not pleased with the President's decision. They thought such a meeting would validate the perception that President Barack Obama's government supported the opposition in Zambia.

The opposition of course capitalized on the good publicity and posted pictures all over the internet showing Sata and Clinton in a meeting at the US embassy in Lusaka. She also met the leader of the second biggest opposition party, Hakainde Hichilema of the United Party for National Development (UPND).

The party had also raised concerns with the continuous voter registration exercise ahead of the elections. Some senior party members tried in vain to convince the President not to allow the exercise to continue in an election year.

"First time voters usually vote for the opposition," one party official said.

The President disagreed and allowed the process to go on and many young people got on the voters' roll for the first time.

The final register was readily available at a fee to candidates, political parties, election monitors and journalists.

"I promised to run a clean election," he often said.

"I don't want to have the tag of rigging elections on my head," he added.

The rigging allegations against the President were extended to the media.

In the pre-election period, the media became polarized too. The opposition argued that rigging started with the manipulation of the state media.

The government owned two daily newspapers, *Times of Zambia* and *Zambia Daily Mail*, which completely went pro-governing party and the President. The only private daily, *The Post*, was for the opposition PF from the onset.

In the electronic media, the state-run public broadcaster, *Zambia National Broadcasting Corporation* (ZNBC) threw its support for governing party while the other private television stations tried to balance their coverage. ZNBC aired a series of documentaries: "Stand Up for Zambia" by freelance producer, Chanda Chimba, which were widely seen as aimed at discrediting the opposition and particularly the PF, the Catholic Church and other vocal critics of the President ahead of the elections.

The station ran a number of ads of the President, which I had placed earlier in the year. When parliament was dissolved and the election date announced, I issued instructions to pull them down to allow for the paid-for political ones to be aired.

The small community radio stations gave coverage to any candidate or party that paid for the programmes.

"Remove them, I don't want to be accused of abusing ZNBC," the President said when I sought his permission.

"And make sure all campaign adverts by our members are paid for by them," he instructed.

The President and the governing party were accused of abusing the state-run media to champion their campaigns in breach of the electoral code of conduct.

I was singled out by the opposition as one of the architects of the media bias of the state-owned media.

Some opposition members nicknamed me "Goebbels" in reference to Hitler's Minister of Propaganda Paul Joseph Goebbels.

At one press conference, the PF spokesman Given Lubinda alleged that I was personally writing editorials in the state-run newspapers and that I determined headlines from State House.

'This is the work of Dickson Jere. We have evidence," Lubinda said while waving a copy of the *Zambia Daily Mail*, which had a negative story on him and Sata.

But that was not true. I never wrote even a single story during my State House days.

Sata occasionally texted or called me to complain against the perceived biased media coverage.

"*Iwe ka* (small) Jere, tell your people to stop writing bad things about me," Sata would say.

I had known him as my 'good news source' when I worked as a reporter. He was a minister in the government of President Chiluba then before he quitting to form his own party.

Even though the state-run papers were seen to be biased, they had become less effective in terms of influencing readers. We had even planned to privatize one of the newspapers so that a credible investor could takeover. During this time, I even travelled to Nairobi to meet the owner of *The Nation* Group, the Aga Khan and his management at the newspaper, which was expanding into other African countries. However, the process in Zambia took long as we had to go through formal lengthy privatization.

******

The public outcry against media bias and in particular the state-run broadcaster intensified. This prompted lawyers under the auspices of the Law Association of Zambia (LAZ) to commence public interest litigation against ZNBC on the grounds of bias and unethical conduct in election reporting. The lawyers argued that ZNBC was financed by the national treasury as well as television levies which were paid by Zambians regardless of political affiliation.

The legal challenge was only dropped after ZNBC made an undertaking to abide by the law and provide equal coverage to all candidates.

A number of different newspapers mushroomed during the election campaign which is the usual trend in Zambia ahead of elections. They supported different candidates and political parties although their influence over voters was limited. The only new aspect was the online publication, the *Zambian Watchdog*, which proved to be popular during the run-up to the elections. It was a free online newspaper that provided updates on the political goings on in Zambia.

It was accessed mainly on mobile telephones and the internet in urban areas. Internet penetration in rural areas remained patchy.

The publication tried to give balanced coverage although with a strong slant towards the UPND.

Can we place the President's advert in The Post? was the question that stirred debate among us. There were strong views from both sides. I was among those who felt we should advertise in the newspaper despite it being critical of the President.

"The end justifies the means," I said.

The campaign team wanted to reach out to opposition supporters and most of them read that newspaper religiously. So to me it seemed there was no other option if they were to be reached.

"How can we give money to the enemy to continue fighting us?" was the question I was frequently asked in those discussions.

After weighting the pros and cons, the meeting resolved to place some ads in the 'opposition newspaper'.

******

As the campaigns heated up, the opposition started making wild allegations.

The main contender, Michael Sata, started portraying himself as the President-in-waiting. He said that the army commander and other top security chiefs had started reporting to him even before elections.

This riled the defence chiefs. In an unprecedented move in the history of the country, they held a news conference.

"Don't involve us in partisan politics. We are loyal to the government of the day and the Commander in-Chief," said army commander Lt-General Wisdom Lopa, who was flanked by the commanders of the Air force and the Zambia National Service.

In the political arena, there was last minute horse-trading between the governing party and the UPND for a possible loose alliance. Initially the UPND was in a pact with the PF but the two broke ranks just before the elections.

The UPND and its leader Hichilema had strong regional support in the Southern province, which had a high number of registered voters. If Hichilema pulled out of the race and backed the President victory would be certain.

The UPND demanded a constitutional amendment to include a 50 percent plus one vote threshold for the presidential vote. The prediction was that no single candidate could garner the majority vote and a second round was envisaged where UPND could back the President.

"The talks came down to issues of trust," one official involved in the discussions said.

After back and forth discussions, the talks broke down and the two parties went their separate ways.

The President had to fight the battle on his own although some smaller political parties backed him. They included the National Democratic Front and the United Liberal Party.

The 2011 elections were tripartite in nature: presidential, parliamentary and local government. But the concentration came to be on the presidential race.

There was a delay in choosing candidates for the MMD. The party did not have a primary elections system for picking candidates. Aspirants were interviewed and chosen by a small panel of officials. The process was nearly always acrimonious.

Veteran politician and MMD strategist Vernon Mwaanga had pushed in vain to have the selection done early.

"It allows the party to heal," he said.

"It also gives chance to make amends in cases where the wrong candidate is picked," he argued.

Candidates chosen by the lower organs of the party could be disqualified by the national executive committee if indications were that the wrong one was chosen.

This time around, the process was not well handled in some parts of the country. In Lusaka for instance, the party had no credible candidates and ended up fielding former opposition lawmakers at the last minute.

Some of those who were not picked but felt were popular either stood as independents or joined the opposition. That weakened the party in some areas and consequently affected the presidential poll as voters tended to vote along party lines.

CHAPTER SEVENTEEN
STABILITY, SECURITY AND PROSPERITY

The President flagged off his official campaign on August 7, 2011 at the Hotel Intercontinental in Lusaka. The banquet hall was full of diplomats, journalists, the clergy, election observers and civil society groups.

His campaign team proved equal to the demands of the occasion.

The planning had been meticulous. It was to be the most powerful and unique election campaign ever.

It was well funded with a surfeit of campaign materials.

Children were treated to lollipops branded with the President's portrait. Households had free bulbs with his portrait. There were MMD-branded coffee mugs for offices, watches and flags - all in navy blue and white – the colours of the governing MMD. Street poles and trees were draped in MMD campaign posters.

Hundreds of vehicles hit the roads across the country, all branded with the campaign line – "A President for all Zambians". University and college students had fancy caps and T-shirts with badges with the president's portrait. The candidate at times abandoned his usual presidential motorcade and jumped on what came to be known as the "Battle Bus," a 64-seater Higer luxury coach, which was branded with his photos and slogans.

Many observers said that it unfolded as a western-style campaign.

A new campaign website went up, followed by a YouTube channel, twitter account and a Facebook page for the President. A pre-recorded voicemail message from the President hit thousands of mobile telephone subscribers while text messages systematically went viral on the social media. Radio and television adverts were placed on both state-run and private stations.

The packages were professionally done and were not typical of an African election campaign.

I was part of the team that worked on the social media strategies and on broadcast ads. It was a lot of work to keep the President on script during recordings. The crew was strict, any slight mistake or noise meant redoing the whole shoot. It was irritating at times.

But the best results were achieved.

The opposition seemed to have no chance from the outset. They faced a powerful, well-coordinated and organized campaign and immediately it got underway most people thought it was game over for the opposition.

"Only MMD can deliver security, stability and prosperity for all Zambians," the President told the launch and there were attainments to go by.

Under his leadership, Zambia had become a food basket for Africa, exporting food to the Democratic Republic of Congo, Kenya, Malawi and Zimbabwe.

"Together we managed to produce unprecedented maize harvests for two years. Together, we managed to establish a stable fuel supply and for the first time –uniform fuel pricing across the country," the President said, citing his record in office.

The main opposition party the Patriotic Front (PF) hit back more or less immediately.

It filed an urgent application for an injunction to restrain the President from distributing campaign materials with immediate effect on the grounds that they were acquired using either stolen funds from the treasury or from dubious sources. According to the affidavit in support sworn by the PF General Secretary, Wynter Kabimba, there was no evidence that import duties had been paid on the materials.

He also asked the court for an investigation into possible money laundering by the governing party. It said the money that the party used to buy 100 vans, over 5,000 bicycles and an undisclosed number of abrasive T-shirts, caps and bicycles was not legally obtained.

The President assembled a crack team of lawyers. It was led by veteran lawyer and academician Professor Patrick Mvunga, former Minister at State House Eric Silwamba.. He worked with Christopher Mundia who ran a practice in Lusaka. The team responded and argued that there was no law compelling candidates to disclose the source of their funding just as there was none limiting the amounts of money to be spent on an election.

After a hearing, the court threw out the application paving way for the campaign.

"Since there is no law in existence which requires a political party to disclose income and source, I accordingly find that there is no cause of action in relation to this relief," said Judge Florence Lengalenga in her ruling of September 13, 2011.

The President was invited for a 'live debate' with other presidential candidates. The show was sponsored by the BBC and the United Nations Development Programme (UNDP) to discuss the manifestos. When we heard that the main challenger Sata was not going to appear, we also abandoned the debate. It was pointless to debate with candidates who had little chance of winning the polls, which were widely expected to be a two horserace.

We went back to our campaign schedule.

The initial plan was for the President to tour all the 150 parliamentary constituencies in a period of five weeks. But time was tight. A new flexible timetable had to be worked out between State House aides and his campaign team.

Two choppers and two planes were strictly dedicated to the President and his team's use. I was to be with him at every campaign meeting.

It had all the makings of a hectic five weeks!

In a day, we targeted at least three meetings.

Lunch was a luxury. The usual food on the campaign helicopters came to be mainly fruits.

I worked together with the foreign consultants, prepared short speeches for every meeting that the candidate addressed. The President had one message, which we localized to suit the area we were in.

It was that he stood for "security, stability and prosperity for all Zambians" and for "building tomorrow's Zambia."

"We want jobs! We want jobs! We want jobs!" the job-hungry youths chanted when they saw the Presidential motorcade in the opposition stronghold - the Copperbelt province.

The President ordered the motorcade to stop. But the youths ran away when they saw the heavily armed police officers, part of the entourage, jumping out of the vanettes.

"Come back, come back...," the President called out.

Few had the courage to approach. He engaged those who did in conversation and in no time at all, a huge crowd of noisy youths surrounded the President, jostling to shake his hand.

He was clearly in campaign mode as he talked to them.

"*Ndiye Campaign iyi*! (This is the campaign)" the President would say on a number of occasions after a whistle-stop.

He insisted rallies and organized town hall meetings were only for boosting morale since the people who usually attended were mainly party members or the already converted.

Markets were also the President's favorite. He mingled with marketers and bought basic foodstuffs from them.

But the security detail was posing some unforeseen problems.

The more he made whistle-stops, the more aggressive they became: pushing around the would-be voters! At times the President lost his temper and shouted at them to allow the people approach. But they would not listen – they had a duty to protect the President of the Republic of Zambia and Commander In-Chief of the Armed Forces regardless of the campaign.

After the first week, a post-mortem was called. The consensus was that the campaign had started off well but was marred by the presence of uniformed and heavily armed police surrounding the candidate. Some people were scared to walk and talk to the President after seeing the guns and bullets.

It was proposed that a meeting with the police command should be organized to resolve the issue.

"Dickson, give them the orders, no need for meetings," the President said.

I was the only government employee present in the meeting.

The rest were consultants, volunteers, party officials and members of the first family.

I was not about to start a fight with the "system" again. I had fought a long battle with them over two years on the ever-present armed police around the President.

"I will take it up sir," I said, paving way for the meeting to discuss more substantial issues.

I discussed the concerns raised with the security people after the meeting. Initially, they refused to pay heed. On further discussion a compromise was reached. They promised to use more bodyguards in "civvies" during the campaign period.

"They should even wear campaign materials," I joked with them after the agreement was reached.

The police made some adjustments when the next round of campaigning started.

I was squeezed in between two State House aides in a tiny Agusta helicopter. Instead of the designated four passengers, we were six, heading for a meeting in the Northern Province.

It was a two-hour trip and was very bumpy and uncomfortable.

"The President better win these elections," I said to break the long silence on board.

My colleagues supported me in unison.

We had stopped wearing the office suits in that five-week period and at times wore campaign attire too.

My group was the advance party for the President.

He trailed us with a bigger, more comfortable and faster helicopter.

Sometimes they overtook us midair and would later circle the landing strip for some time to allow us to land first.

Helicopters were good for the campaign. They could land anywhere but more importantly they attracted crowds in the more remote parts.

"Most people have refused to attend the meeting because they didn't receive any campaign materials," one senior party official reported.

The materials, especially those in the form of clothing, were new and came in handy for the poor. They were much in demand and some party officials who received them had the tendency to distribute the stuff to a close-knit circle excluding many party supporters.

"The materials are becoming a curse to the campaign," I told the President.

He laughed because we never thought we would encounter such problems. Infighting was to intensify over the campaign materials. Not enough were reaching the outlying areas where the voters lived.

I noted down the complaints.

"Get some materials from the plane and distribute them," the President directed.

He always carried some with him for distribution during impromptu stops.

When the bale of T-shirts was offloaded from the chopper, there was a mad rush for them and the meeting turned chaotic.

"Please give them after the meeting," he now said after having had to pause in his address as a result of the commotion.

The opposition took advantage of the growing confusion and frustration over the campaign materials. The PF told Zambians to demand them because they were bought from "stolen" public funds.

"Get the T-shirts, get the caps, wear them every day but on the 20th vote wisely," Michael Sata would tell Zambians, referring to September 20, 2011, the polling day.

He coined his campaign slogan *"Don't Kubeba"*, slang for 'Don't tell them!'

Demand for the materials increased as opposition members also joined the fray.

In the midst of the campaign, the team temporarily suspended the distribution of the materials, an act that angered party members. I was not privy to the reasons but I raised the matter with the President.

Various opinion polls, including our internal one, showed positive results for the President in the weeks of September. He had picked up and was ahead of his archrival Sata by a small margin. He needed to sustain the campaign by focusing on his achievements over the three-years of his tenure and avoid having to wage a negative campaign about his opponents.

We had areas of concentration designated the 'priority provinces' where the President was scheduled to spend more time.

"I will visit all the provinces, I don't want to be accused of neglecting any part of the country," he said.

He was not comfortable with the idea of touching some provinces for a day while spending more time in priority provinces, which included Eastern, Western, Northern, Lusaka, Central and Copperbelt provinces. Northwestern was a stronghold of the President, but the voter concentration was low. The remaining two, Luapula and Southern provinces had remained significantly in opposition hands. Going by our opinion poll, there was little our efforts could have done to change the voting pattern going.

******

Political rallies were very exciting.

Multitudes of people converged to see the President. Others were attracted by the live music performed by leading local musicians. There were fewer and shorter speeches but a lot more singing and dancing. The President and his wife would occasionally take to the floor to the excitement of the crowd.

The scenes were carnival-like. Some party supporters painted their faces navy blue and white while others blew the *vuvuzela* - the noisy plastic horns.

Comedians took to the stage to entertain the crowds. There was never a dull moment.

"Victory is certain," the President declared.

His speeches were always interjected by loud music in his praise.

"This is how the campaign should be. The young, old and even children are here to enjoy," the President told the cheering crowds.

At 74, he looked young and energetic for his age. He occasionally made a political jibe at his opponents saying he was campaigning for re-election while physically fit after hiring a personal trainer.

"The President is very strong. He doesn't get tired," said one female journalist who was in the delegation.

She was knackered after attending four different rallies in a day without rest or food.

Some pockets of violence began to surface slowly as the campaign gained momentum. Interparty clashes heightened in Lusaka and the Copperbelt where the opposition was strong. The media blamed the governing party, especially in Lusaka where the party chairman William Banda was singled out.

Our assessment showed that violence in these two areas was discrediting the President. The opinion polls indicated that respondents believed that the governing party was causing the violence. In some cases, we had tangible evidence that it had been instigated by the opposition but nevertheless the blame was on the President.

"This must be stopped forthwith," one election advisor said.

"The violent acts are taking away the positive attributes of the President," he said.

Soon the President's rating steadily dropped in those two provinces.

The church, civil society and diplomats joined in condemning the violence and called on the police to act.

Gruesome pictures of people hacked or beaten were shown on television and in newspapers, and the story was always that they were victims of MMD violence.

"Arrest whoever is perpetrating violence regardless of the political party they belong to" the President ordered the police.

Further, he summoned the MMD Lusaka provincial chairman for a meeting where the latter was instructed to end the violence.

"Even if you are provoked, just walk away," the President said.

I took this opportunity to explain the political repercussions of the violence to the Lusaka MMD leadership. But even as polling day approached the violence continued in some areas, unabated.

At the end of the five weeks of campaigning, the President had flown 19 hours, 40 minutes, equivalent to 9,125 kilometers in his fixed wing presidential plane, while he flew 60 hours or 16,200 kilometers with the presidential helicopter. It was hectic and involved sleeping in tents and military cantonments in some places. I was with the President on every one of those engagements.

The campaign period ended on September 17, 2011 - two days before polling day.

The President had the last rally in Mandevu, a densely populated slum in Lusaka. It was one of the biggest rallies ever seen. It was the sixtieth rally.

The crowds ecstatically waved flags to the President as he arrived in the 'Battle Bus' with his aides and family members, all clad in party regalia.

"The MMD is the only party with a clear vision and direction," the President told the crowd.

He cited the new road project, dubbed 'formula one' that he had started to open the country through infrastructure development.

"I am sure I am winning," he declared.

Supporters had lined up the main roads leading to the rally waving and dancing.

It was a fantastic way to end the campaign - on a high note.

The following day, we were back at State House and wanted the President to get back to his usual schedule of attending to national duties.

The President was scheduled to officially open the ultramodern stadium in Ndola, which was constructed during his tenure.

"Opening the stadium amounts to campaigning," the opposition complained to the Electoral Commission of Zambia (ECZ).

They argued that it gave the President an unfair advantage to officiate at public functions after the campaign period had closed.

"He is going there as Head of State and not as a presidential candidate," I tried to draw the distinction when the ECZ informed me of the complaint.

I had already announced that the President was scheduled to launch the new sports facility in Ndola, an opposition stronghold.

The President was also scheduled to open the newly constructed government Conference Centre at the Government Complex in Lusaka. These events were planned well in advanced but we put them on hold in those five weeks to allow the President concentrate on the campaigns.

I went to see the President to inform him about the opposition concerns. He was at home relaxing in the gardens when we met.

"I thought you were resting at home. That was a hectic programme," he said referring to the campaign.

"Thank you for being there with me," he said as he offered me a seat.

I informed him of the complaint.

"Just cancel everything; I don't want to be accused of interfering with the elections. Let the best candidate win," he said.

That is how the two projects, which were constructed during his tenure, were never officially opened by him. He simply passed them over.

I was back in my office. I knew the race was too close to call. I was privy to the results of our internal opinion polls that clearly showed a neck-to-neck race even in the last week of the campaign. I packed my personal belongings in carton boxes and put them in my vehicle.

The Chief of Staff Dr. Austin Sichinga asked everyone to clear their outstanding work before the elections. I was unable to do that since I had accompanied the President on the campaign trail. Thus, the two days came in handy as I used them to clear my desk.

A day before elections, I was ready for any eventuality.

Even though I was a public officer employed by government, I knew I could not work with the new President as spokesman if my 'boss' lost. I was too much in his inner circle and could not betray his trust.

CHAPTER EIGHTEEN
THE LAST MANIFEST

"This could be the last manifest," joked Bob Samakai, the President's Chief of Protocol, when we boarded a Zambia Air Force presidential plane for Chipata on September 20, 2011.

A manifest is the document in aviation that contains the names and total number of passengers on the flight. The chief of protocol used to be the custodian of the manifest and prepared it for every trip. Allowances on presidential trips were paid based on the manifest, and the manifest for a presidential trip was a confidential document in the civil service.

It was polling day.

I woke up around 04:30 hours to cast my vote early at a polling station situated outside State House. I wanted to be the first on the queue as I was among the aides to accompany the President to his hometown of Chipata where he was to cast his vote.

When I reached the polling station, I found a very long queue. Luckily, many of them were State House workers and their families. So, they allowed me to jump the queue and vote. I was among the first three voters when the station opened at 06:00 hours. Agents of all participating political parties as well as local and foreign election monitors were on hand to observe the voting.

After voting, I proceeded to my office briefly and later to Nkhwazi House to check on the President.

I found him geared and ready to go to vote. He was registered in his hometown.

"What time are we leaving?" he asked.

I told him we had set takeoff at 07:30 hours.

"Make sure the NRC (National Registration Card) and the voter's card are together," I said, just to make sure that he had the two documents required for voting.

Without any of the two cards, one cannot vote in Zambia.

"Ah, you have voted already?" the President commented as I lifted my index finger to show the indelible ink used to identify voters who had cast their ballot.

Other State House aides and close presidential security officers had also voted and were ready to take the boss and his wife on the hour-long flight to Chipata. In Zambia, one may vote only at the polling station where one is registered.

The President arrived at the City Airport air force base.

He was not with his usual long presidential motorcade. He only had about five cars in the convoy. Other security and support staff had been released to go and cast their votes. There is no provision for early voting for security and other essential workers.

The defence and security commanders saluted as he alighted from his official Mercedes Benz with his wife.

He looked serious as he greeted the Generals who had lined up to welcome him at the military base.

Within ten minutes, the propeller engined plane was taxing for takeoff.

"The last manifest," the President's senior private secretary said, prompting laughter on the plane.

When ascending, we could see through the small windows of the plane thousands of people in various polling stations in queues waiting to vote. It looked like there would be high voter turnout.

"Dickson, look at the people," the President said.

I was the only one who knew what he meant.

In our assessment based on the internal opinion polls, we had anticipated a high voter turnout in 'priority areas' based on the assumption that a lower turnout would favor the opposition.

The hour-long flight was like any other local trip. There were jokes, laughter and arguments over almost anything. The Chief of Staff, Dr. Sichinga, was the all-rounder when it came to knowledge. He lectured us on stuff ranging from aviation, plants, soils, and animals to water, energy and food. Sometimes we disagreed with him just to keep him talking.

When we were descending towards Chipata, there were no visible queues in the villages and nearby towns. It was in sharp contrast to what we saw when ascending.

I went quiet for a moment and looked tense.

"What's wrong my brother?' Samakai asked after noticing that my usual boisterous character had suddenly changed.

"Look, there are no voters here," I said, although I knew he didn't know what I meant. He was not part of the opinion poll team.

The team was a small group that met with the President at his residence. The assessment indicated that Eastern Province, the President's stronghold, needed a high voter turnout for him to be certain of victory.

What I saw through the window was not reassuring.

It dawned on me at that moment that this could indeed be the "last manifest."

We landed and found only about four vehicles mobilized from government departments. The President and his wife used one vehicle while the rest shared with bodyguards the remaining three. The usual security sweepers and sirens were absent. There was no advance party as the presidential motorcade remained in Lusaka.

"Where are the voters?" the President asked the party officials who welcomed him.

They tried to convince him that it was too early for villagers and turnout would improve from the latter part of the morning.

It was not a convincing explanation but nevertheless the President gave them the benefit of the doubt. But experience showed that rural voters usually cast their ballots early in the morning.

We proceeded to the polling station where the First Lady voted and later to the President's polling station. He was casually dressed as he walked to a primary school, greeting children who had turned up to catch a glimpse of him.

At around 10:00 hours, there was no single person on the queue and this was supposed to be the President's backyard in terms of votes.

"Some people don't want to vote because they know President Rupiah Banda has already won these elections," one party official told us.

Journalists had travelled the 600 kilometres by road from Lusaka to cover the President voting. He cast his vote while photographers jostled for shots. He later took questions from journalists before retiring for breakfast at a private lodge.

While on the road, my mobile telephone rang.

"There is a problem here (Lusaka) and the Copperbelt,' said Lt. General Ronnie Shikapwasha, the outgoing Minister of Information and MMD chairman for security.

"Tell the President the opposition is disrupting voting and is rioting in some polling stations," he said, emphasizing that the message was 'very urgent'.

I briefed the President and the Chief of Staff.

In no time, he was on a call to the police chief.

"We can't allow the country to go up in flames just because of elections," I could hear him say on the phone.

More calls came through from different sources saying the violence was getting out of hand in Lusaka and the Copperbelt. In some areas, the riots were sparked by rumors of pre-marked ballot papers for the President.

The late opening of some polling stations also created confusion.

After breakfast, we headed for the airport en-route to Lusaka. We spent nearly two hours in Chipata before flying back.

The flight this time around was bumpy due to high humidity. It was very hot.

The President consulted on how to handle the violence. There was a suggestion that the army be deployed on the streets of Lusaka and the Copperbelt if the situation degenerated further but he tossed that idea out.

"We have enough policemen to deal with the situation. Perpetrators of violence are just a small group," he said.

When we got back to the office, more reports filtered in. The riots were steadily spreading in the slums.

In the densely populated Matero constituency in Lusaka, stone-throwing youths set burning tyres in the streets, smashed cars, blocked roads and stoned riot police.

"It's becoming very difficult. There are boxes without covers, papers without serial numbers and so on," Sata told journalists.

His interview was constantly repeated on private radio and television stations. It only worsened the situation as riot police continued the running battles with the unruly mobs supporting the opposition PF.

The privately owned *Muvi TV* station ran live commentaries and pictures of alleged rigging attempts in some areas. The broadcasts incited further demonstrations in Lusaka and the Copperbelt.

I took up the issue with the proprietor of the station.

"Please tone down those reports. You will put the country on fire," I told Steve Nyirenda, the owner of the station.

"*Zambia election – violence, riots erupt,*" was the breaking news alert from the international newswire, AFP. The story was also making headlines on CNN, Reuters and BBC.

"A riot erupted on Tuesday in one of the Zambian capital's most populated slums, after opposition supporters claimed they found a man carrying pre-marked ballot papers for national elections now under way," the story said.

International monitoring groups tried to calm the situation down saying they had not detected anything of that sort.

We had anticipated violence on polling day but not to the extent that was emerging. Intelligence reports indicated that the opposition was planning a "Kenya Formula" if the vote went against them. The formula referred to the 2007 bloody post-election violence in the East African country where hundreds of people were killed and thousands more displaced.

In Zambia, some opposition supporters had armed themselves with machetes, knives, axes, sjamboks and slingshots.

The President, in a televised address before voting day, tried to pre-empt the planned violence and warned perpetrators of stiff punishment.

"There has been much rumour and I hope it is just rumour that there will be violence," he said in the September 18, 2011 national address, just two days before voting.

"To those who may be contemplating illegal acts or intimidation or even worse physical violence...I have ordered the police to arrest and prosecute all those who offend," the President said.

He had used the address to declare the polling day a national holiday in order to allow as many voters as possible to cast their vote.

The President also reiterated his position that he would accept the result whichever way it went.

"I can only speak for myself and my party when I say that we will abide by the results. I hope that all other parties contesting the elections will also pledge to abide by the final results," he said.

By afternoon, the violence had receded.

The police had managed to quell the riots and voters were back on the queues. The polling stations that were temporarily closed due to violence reopened.

Election officials announced that instead of voting closing at 18:00 hours, the designated time, voters who were on the queue by that time would still be allowed to vote.

Rigging rumours were widespread across the country on voting day although there was violence only in Lusaka and the Copperbelt.

Some voters refused to use the pen provided by the ECZ for marking the ballot papers. Election officials allowed the skeptical ones to use their pens. There was a belief spread that pens provided by the ECZ had ink that faded when one voted opposition and such a vote was spoilt.

The leading opposition candidate Sata toured polling stations in what came to be perceived as last minute campaigning. The President's agents complained to the ECZ saying that Sata was constantly lifting his fist – the symbol of his party-whenever he visited polling stations. It was illegal as the law in Zambia prohibited campaigning within 400-metre radius of the polling stations.

"We will also ask the President to do the same," the MMD told ECZ.

Candidates were allowed to check on voting in selected polling stations but not to engage in campaigns.

I received a call from the President's election agent Mikatazo Wakumelo.

"The boss should also start going round the polling stations," he said.

"Not necessary," I responded.

We, at State House, had discussed that issue the day before and the President had outrightly refused to tour polling stations. He said he wanted voters to be free to choose their preferred candidates without undue influence.

Later the ECZ received the formal complaint from the MMD and eventually stopped Sata's tours.

Most polling stations closed as scheduled at 18:00 hours.

Counting immediately began at the polling stations. The results were later transmitted for tallying at the main centre – the Mulungushi International Conference Centre in Lusaka.

******

I was home early monitoring the slow pace of the results. I made several calls to the campaign centre to follow up on the latest results.

The President phoned me several times to check if I had picked up some more results.

I realized that the campaign team had made a serious mistake when they failed to give me results straight from the polling stations across the country. They did not have polling agents with mobile phones to communicate results directly to the campaign center. They relied on updates from the official ECZ results. I couldn't believe that there could be such an omission by the team when they had run a successful and well-organized campaign.

I went to bed early but could not sleep. I had serious insomnia.

My phone kept ringing with calls from different people either to give me updated results or asking me for the latest figures.

By midnight, word began to go round that the President had lost and that the ECZ had given him the final tally before the official announcement.

Press queries over the same flooded by incoming emails.

The President telephoned.

"We have to do something about these reports making the rounds. These unverified results may cause problems for the country," he said.

The situation in the country was relatively calm as people waited for the final results. The few results that were released came from urban areas where the opposition was in the lead as expected.

I suggested issuing a press statement the following morning to respond to reports that the President had received the final results showing that he had lost.

"President Banda is not aware of the final results that are still being compiled and will, like anyone else, wait for the ECZ to announce the results," I said in a press release of September 21, 2011.

"We know there are people who are trying to create anarchy by taking advantage of the situation. Zambians should remain calm and wait for the final results from the ECZ," I said.

Fake results appeared on the ECZ website showing that Sata had won.

Celebrations began in some parts of the country when they saw the so-called official final results. At that time, counting was still on.

I phoned the ECZ chairperson Justice Mambilima to countercheck on the results posted on the official website.

"Ignore those results. Our website has been hacked," she said, calmly.

She said her office was going to issue a public statement on the hacking of the website and that people should only take as official the results that she personally announced at intervals. She had up to that point only announced 33 constituencies out of the 150 but the results on the website showed 133 constituencies counted.

"The ECZ website has been tampered with and fake results posted to mislead the nation," Mambilima told a news briefing.

"We have since suspended the results component of the website pending investigations on the matter," she said.

The delay in announcing the results triggered fresh protests in the capital and the Copperbelt. Opposition youths suspected that the ECZ was conniving with the President to steal the votes.

They blocked roads and marched on the streets calling for the results to be released. The commission had anticipated announcing final results within 48 hours but logistical problems in reaching far-flung areas caused the delay.

"The commission hopes to receive all the results within a reasonable time-frame," Justice Mambilima promised the nation in a televised address.

"We urge media houses not to speculate but allow the commission to complete its work of processing the results," she said in apparent reference to *The Post*, which reported that Sata had won.

The final results were now due to be announced at around 22:00 hours that night. But when the time came, there was no announcement. It caused panic.

By that time, most of us at State House had known the outcome through intelligence sources. The President was aware too. He had lost the election.

"We have not crossed," said Chief of Staff when I met him at the office, and he advised us to prepare handover notes.

The President phoned me to check if I had heard the results.

"We can't catch up," I said to him when I relayed the information.

There was still counting going on but not from enough constituencies to offset the difference.

"Start working on the conceding speech," he said.

His political advisory team insisted that their figures showed that he had closed the gap and the vote could swing either way with the remaining polling stations. I didn't agree and the President didn't as well. It was simple arithmetic. Even if the President won all the remaining votes, the gap would still be yawning.

My phone rang. It was a surprise call.

"Our results show that the President has lost. Is he going to concede?" was the question from a close-friend Joe Kaunda, then news editor of *The Post*.

"The President is going to concede and between you and me, he has already conceded defeat," I answered.

"But...," I interjected and told my friend to wait for the official results and the position of the President would be known.

By midnight of the third day after voting, the official results were announced.

Sata received 1,150,45 votes or 43 percent while the President only managed to garner 961,796 or 36.1 percent.

The Chipata trip was indeed the last manifest for all of us.

It was game over!

I called the Secretary to the Cabinet to request that the swearing in ceremony should be delayed for few hours to allow the President address the nation. I wanted my boss to have a dignified send-off by having a live address to the nation.

"Let's allow him to have the press conference in the morning and thereafter swearing in ceremony," I said.

The Secretary to Cabinet agreed.

CHAPTER NINETEEN
DON'T KILL THE MESSENGER

Bang! Bang! Bang! There was huge noise at my gate.

The armed police officer guarding my home came to my bedroom window to alert me of the mob of unruly youths who had marched on my house. I lived in the quiet Lusaka neighbourhood of Chudleigh.

Supporters of the Patriotic Front (PF), which had just won the presidential election, marched from a nearby slum as part of their victory celebrations. But they were violent, possibly drunk and continued to bang on my gate while others threw stones and other objects onto my rooftop. They even emptied the rubbish bins at the entrance.

It was scary. I didn't know how to respond.

"What do they want?" I asked the police officer.

"I don't know Sir," he said as he asked me if he could fire warning shots in the air to disperse them.

I discouraged him. I thought the sound gun fire would only aggravate the already volatile situation.

"*Pabwato* (on the boat)" they chanted the PF slogan as they continued banging on the gate.

My five bull dogs scampered around the yard, barking aimlessly as the noise intensified in the early morning.

My children were awoken by the noise and I didn't know what to tell them as they started crying.

Some of my neighbours joined in the celebrations by sounding the *vuvuzela*s.

I had just arrived home after working on the president's farewell speech.

I knew the President had lost after we got preliminary results through the intelligence. The President knew too. I was not there when he was informed of the results but I understand he was shocked before he regained composure.

"Well, the people have spoken," he was reported to have said after a long pause.

The nation was glued to television and radio waiting for the result of the presidential election.

I told my family the result before I went to bed.

I sent out invitations for a press conference the following morning at State House as I left the office for home. Nobody knew the reasons for the early morning press conference but speculation abounded. The President knew he had lost and wanted to dispute the results, as is the trend in Africa.

******

The police officer was back at my window.

"I have asked for reinforcements Sir," he said.

He thought the mob was too unruly and could enter the premises with unknown consequences.

The *Zambian Watchdog* broke the story first.

"PF cadres have attacked the house of Dickson Jere, the State House spokesman, following the announcement of the results," read the story.

I was the target because I issued statements against Sata when he was in opposition. The opposition targeted prominent names around the outgoing President. The MMD party spokesperson Dora Siliya's house, near State House, was for instance a target too but police drove the marauding youths away.

The Lusaka MMD chairman William Banda's house was ransacked. PF supporters took away everything and threw some of his clothes on the roads as they danced on them in supposed celebration.

As the noise continued outside my gate, I gained composure. I picked my mobile phone and called the number of the President-elect.

I wanted him to intervene and order his supporters off.

That morning I was due to report early at the office in readiness for the press conference. His mobile phone was off.

Damn it, I sighed.

I put in the next call to his eldest son, Mulenga, who was a friend. Luckily, he answered. But before I could explain in detail he passed the handset on to his father.

"Speak to your uncle," he said.

There was a brief pause and I could hear his father talking in the background.

Iwe ka (small) Jere, where are you?" he asked and before I could respond he was offering me a job.

"I want you to be my press secretary..." the line abruptly cut before he could finish.

His son re-dialed and gave the phone back to his father.

"Where are you? You come home," he said before I interjected and explained my reasons for calling.

He listened attentively before he cut in.

"That will be sorted out. But come, you come home," he said before hanging up.

I politely declined the job offer.

I thought it would not be the right thing to do when the President needed those of us who were close to him most. It was also my view that the new President needed his own team.

Suddenly, the noise outside my gate receded.

"They have gone Sir," the police officer reported.

Two small light trucks came to fetch them. I realized it must have been a planned 'visit'.

An hour later, Professor Nkandu Luo, the newly elected Member of Parliament for Munali Constituency, where my home is, telephoned.

"I have just been instructed by the President (Sata) to make sure that you are safe," she said.

"Are the cadres still there?" she asked.

I informed her that they had just left. She gave me her numbers and that of the PF chairman in the area to alert her should they return.

Sata's son, Mulenga, contacted me again. He wanted to find out if I was fine and whether the unruly youths had dispersed. He was calling on behalf of his father, he said. I remained grateful to him for that gesture which meant a lot to me and my family at that time of uncertainty.

A friend of mine in Europe picked up the story of the attack at my house online and was concerned. He thought he should help me flee the country.

"My brother, pick up the passports and your family," he said without the usual pleasantries we normally exchanged.

He had chartered a jet from Zimbabwe. The plane was ready for the 30-minute flight into Zambia to pick me up and my family.

"But we can't get landing rights. Please push with your connections," he said as he gave me the plane details and the names of the crew.

He wanted me flown to South Africa from where he could organize the Schengen Visa for Europe.

He was from the old European communist block where he suffered political persecution before fleeing. He knew what I was going through, he said.

After deep reflection and consultation with family, I decided to stay. My decision was partly the result of the President elect's positive response in the matter of the mob at my gate.

I thought the victimization could only be temporal.

******

I received telephone calls from three outgoing ministers and one opposition leader who wanted to reach the President with a message.

"He should not concede," they said.

I knew a decision had already been made on that issue and found it pointless to resurrect it with the boss although weeks after we left State House, I did mention the name of one of the callers to him.

With PF vigilantes out of my front door, I was ready to go to State House to perform what was to be my last assignment.

I wore my navy blue, pinstripe suit, which I loved to wear for big occasions. I was to be the master of ceremonies at the much-anticipated press conference by the President as speculation spread that he was not going to concede.

My telephone rang. It was the President.

"Where is my speech?" he asked.

He was not aware of the tribulations that I had faced at home that morning. I didn't want to tell him earlier as I thought he had more serious matters to worry about than cadres storming my home.

"Sorry Sir, I'll come to the office soon," I said as I informed him of the unexpected visitors I had at home.

"Are the children alright?" he asked before assuring me that he would try to speak to the President-elect on the issue the moment he knew his new number.

"I have spoken to him already," I said.

"How?" he asked.

Apparently, he had been looking for the telephone number of the President-elect from the time the results were announced so that he could personally congratulate him and concede defeat. But no one knew the contact number.

"I reached him through his son," I said.

I gave the number to his personal physician who had gone early to Nkhwazi House to check on the President after the results were declared. That is how the President and the President-elect spoke that morning.

******

My short drive to the office was eventful.
Most roads were blocked by youths who lay on their shirts, singing and shouting. They were visibly drunk and in tumult.

"Lift your fist?" they demanded from each motorist before they could clear the way. Even foreign election observers were subjected to the same treatment.

I had to do the same to get passage.

They banged on my car boot while others jumped on top of the roof.

"More money in our pockets, more money in our pockets," they shouted in unison, reciting the campaign promises of Sata.

I had to drive slowly and carefully. I was lucky they didn't recognize me in my dark shades and huge Texas hat.

On some roads, motorists joined in celebrating the end of the 20-year rule of the Movement for Multiparty Democracy (MMD). They drove in a zigzag fashion while honking.

There were similar chaotic scenes in the mining towns of the Copperbelt province, a stronghold of the PF. The celebrations turned ugly when some bars and taverns were looted while government cars were stoned in various slums.

Youths marched on the main highway to the Congo DR border. Some were photographed on top of containers carried by trucks heading for the border.

"*Pabwato! Pabwato! Pabwato!*" they chanted while lifting their fists.

Taxis drove in a single file honking to celebrate the victory in different suburbs. Business was at a standstill as shops and industries closed for the day due to the unpredictable excitement.

Some members of the defeated party were targeted.

They tore MMD campaign T-shirts and caps before setting them on fire to disguise themselves. Some campaigners for the President went into hiding as their homes were ransacked across the country.

Popular Zambian musician Daliso, who sang a lot of songs in praise of the President, was not spared. They burnt his household goods while a comedian, Diffikotti, had his car smashed.

"That's why African leaders do not accept results when they lose," said an African Ambassador who had telephoned to express his commiseration over my ordeal.

The predawn marches to State House organized by the PF youths to evict the President and his family were thwarted by alert police officers. The security had received reports that the opposition planned a march on State House whichever way the vote went. They were prepared for a showdown, as they believed the vote had been rigged well in advance. Police had barricaded the roads leading to State House as armored vehicles and open vans with heavy artillery patrolled the streets around the executive mansion.

That led to speculation that the President would not handover power.

"*We don't want another Gbagbo,*" read a placard carried by one supporter in reference to the former Ivorian President who refused to concede.

"You, Rupiah Banda and his sons are going to jail," read a text message I received as I headed for State House. It was sent by someone known to me who not long ago visited me to lobby for a job in the government.

Another message came from a former junior minister under President Banda.

"You and your Rupiah Banda are going to pay dearly for making MMD lose," he threatened.

I ignored them.

******

When I arrived at the office, I found that only a few workers had reported.

The atmosphere was tense.

The President arrived shortly after me.

When he alighted from his official car, some general workers, in work suits, had lined up at the carport outside his office.

Tears dropped from the eyes of some while others broke down. The President went their direction to bid them goodbye.

"May God look after you," one elderly general worker said as he held the hand of the President tightly.

We sat in his office briefly to go through the speech as the press conference was delayed for over two hours.

The delay increased the speculation. Bloggers talked of a meeting underway involving the President, US Ambassador and the country's first President Kenneth Kaunda. It was said to be urging the President to concede.

That was of course not true.

I was with the President at that moment with the Chief of Staff as we went through the final version of the speech.

When we were done, he briefed me of the discussion he had had with the President-elect after he rang to congratulate him and concede defeat.

"He asked me if I will personally go to the inauguration to handover, I said yes I will be there," the President said.

"I also told him to leave you alone. You were just a messenger. I take full responsibility for whatever statements you issued," the President said and added that the President-elect had promised to protect me from attacks.

"They say don't kill the messenger even if you don't like the message," he said.

The President had also spoken to the incoming first lady Dr. Christine Kaseba to wish her well in her new role.

While discussing we continued to receive reports of systematic attacks on supporters of the President from across the country.

They had the appearance of well-coordinated attacks as the most affected were those seen to have been close to the President.

MMD campaign vehicles were impounded and taken to police stations.

"We have to do something to stop these systematic attacks," he said.

I contacted the parish priest for the St. Ignatius Catholic Church in central Lusaka, Fr. Charles Chilinda, a friend who was also a close-ally of the President-elect. I asked him to help in mobilizing a Church response to end the attacks on innocent people. I also made the same request to Bishop Joshua Banda of the Pentecostal Assemblies of God and asked him to seek an urgent audience with the new leadership over the matter.

They promised to take up the matter.

"In fact I have been trying to get hold of the President-elect over your attack at home," Fr. Chilinda said when I contacted him.

******

The inauguration was set for 10:00 hours the same day the results were announced. Under Zambian law, a new President must be sworn in within 24 hours of being declared the winner. But the President-elect canceled the arrangements at the last minute.

The initial venue for the ceremony was Parliament Buildings but the new team decided to move the ceremony to the Supreme Court and the swearing in ceremony was shifted to the afternoon.

There was a lot of suspicion of the earlier arrangements which were put in place weeks before the election by Cabinet Office. The President-elect canceled all that, including a 21 gun-salute, fly past and a military guard of honor, which had been mounted early in the morning for the new Commander In-chief of the armed forces.

"That was for Rupiah Banda," one senior PF member said.

There was chaos as civil servants had to start making fresh arrangements for the swearing in ceremony within hours. Some invited guests had already taken seats at Parliament Buildings when they were told of the changes.

Some dignitaries who had flown in for the morning event went back without attending the ceremony. Those who returned included Botswana President Lt. General Seretse Ian Khama and Malawian President Professor Bingu Wa Mutharika. The latter was reported to have returned midair.

******

We walked out of the Presidential office to go and meet the press who had gathered from 06:00 hours for the historic press conference.

The President walked with his wife as aides followed in tow.

"Dickson." the President called out to me.

"Please don't go to the swearing in ceremony. Tell Henry too," he said, referring to his son who was involved in the campaign.

"They can hurt you these people," he said as we walked to the banquet hall of State-House to meet the press.

The conference was beamed live on the state-run television.

Was he going to concede defeat? That was the question on everyone's mind and lips.

CHAPTER TWENTY
THE END OF AN ERA

The President sat with his wife on the front table while his senior aides sat behind for solidarity.

This was the usual formation during a presidential address and it was still intact.

The national flag as well as the President's personal standard fluttered on two separate poles right behind the President's chair.

He wore a dark-blue suit, white shirt and a blue and white striped necktie.

A bouquet of fresh roses was on the table where there were dozens of microphones from the press.

A glass of water and tissue on the table were a fixture.

I called the conference to order. We sang the national anthem, and it was now over to him to perform his last task as President.

He flipped through the pages of the speech before he spoke.

He was going to concede defeat.

"The People of Zambia have spoken and we must all listen," the President said as tears rolled down his cheeks.

"We never rigged, we never cheated, we never knowingly abused state funds... we simply did what we thought was best for Zambia," he said.

His voice projection and the sound system in the hall were good.

The President was about to make history.

"I congratulate Michael Sata on his victory," he said as international newswire reporters dashed out to file the breaking news.

It reminded me of my days as a correspondent for AFP when we competed with other news agencies to be the first to break the news.

As the President spoke, my Google alert came on.

"*Tearful Banda concedes defeat*" was the story on the wire reporting that the President had conceded defeat, one of the rare occasions when an African leader willingly bowed out.

"Treat those who you have vanquished with respect and humility that you would expect in your own hour of defeat," he said before breaking down as photographers jostled to take the best shots of the 74 year-old President.

His wife Thandiwe who sat next to him consoled him.

Some of the aides also broke down as he flipped through the speech.

It was the end of the Banda era.

He reflected on the campaign and possible mistakes the party had made.

"Maybe we did not listen, maybe we did not hear," he said.

"Did we become grey and lacking in ideas? Did we lose momentum? Our duty is to go and reflect on any mistakes we may have made and learn from them."

It was a powerful speech, which was widely acclaimed in and outside Zambia. It won the outgoing President a lot of praise and respect.

His political consultants, Bell Pottinger of the UK, wrote the speech. I worked on it with the President shortly before the official results were announced.

In fact, we had two speeches prepared. We were prepared for either way the results could go.

He spoke fluently and thanked Zambians for the opportunity they gave him to serve as President and Commander In-Chief of the armed forces.

"My greatest thanks must go to the Zambian people. We may be a small country in the middle of Africa but we are a great nation. Serving you has been a pleasure and an honor. I wish I could have done more, I wish I had more time," he said.

"Now is not the time for violence and retribution," he said in reference to the various attacks his supporters had been subjected to by the winners.

When he was done with the speech, I stood to take charge of the press conference.

I kept trembling.

"The President will not take questions," I said as some reporters protested.

I didn't want him grilled in the state he was in.

He was too emotional.

I informed the press that the President would be heading to the Supreme Court to personally handover the instruments of power to the President-elect at the inauguration.

We sang the national anthem in closing, as was the tradition at state functions.

He walked out of the banquet hall as the aides followed behind. Camera flashes kept on hitting his face. The photographers wanted to get the last shots of the outgoing President.

He and senior State House staff went into the interview room.

He sat on his usual chair while his wife sat next.

Aides squeezed on the remaining sofas in the small room.

It was time to say goodbyes.

The President conducted a quick roll call, asking everyone whether they were safe.

"It's only Dickson who has been attacked, everyone is safe for now," the Chief of Staff reported.

After a few moments of silence, the President's senior private secretary Robinson Nkonde broke the ice.

"If God asked us to choose another boss, we will still choose you, sir," Nkonde said as most broke down into tears.

The President took out his handkerchief to wipe his.

I looked around the room; it was like a funeral. I was the only one who didn't shed a tear.

"You were very nice to us and you treated us with respect. You guided us where we went wrong. We were like your children," Nkonde said.

The President said he felt sorry for the career civil servants whom he had "poached" from various ministries to work at State House.

"I hope the new President will not sack you. I will speak to him so that you can be taken back to your ministries," he promised.

We all walked out to see him off.

He shook hands with everyone, as he was about to get into his black Mercedes Benz.

"Dickson, please don't come to the inauguration ceremony. It will not be safe for you," he said, reiterating his earlier advice.

He was going home to leave his wife and proceed to the inauguration.

******

I remained at the office with other aides. Only the Chief of Protocol Bob Samakai, his son Andrew and MMD national secretary Major Richard Kachingwe escorted the President to the Supreme Court.

The rest of us followed the event on television.

It was chaotic.

Foreign dignitaries had nowhere to sit. A huge crowd of unruly supporters marched to the Supreme Court almost taking over the show.

They were noisy, unruly and disruptive.

Some carried old bathtubs, which they used to depict the boat, the PF symbol, while others had long sticks as paddles.

When the President arrived, they, surprisingly, gave him a huge round of applause after he had waved to them.

"RB! RB! RB! ..." they shouted his initials.

He sat on a small dais with the President-elect, first President Kenneth Kaunda and the Chief Justice Ernest Sakala, who was the returning officer in the presidential election.

It was also his duty to administer the Oath of Office to the new President.

Justice Sakala handed the Bible to the President-elect as he recited the Oath.

"I Michael Chilufya Sata, having been elected..." the crowd burst into jubilation.

It was the moment they were waiting for!

Others waved placards that read "Man of Action", which was Sata's campaign pitch.

The President handed over to his successor the instruments of power that included the Constitution, the orange Presidential Standard and the Coat of Arms.

He was now officially the former President.

"As we move into this next chapter of Zambia's history, I would like to recognize the peaceful and orderly transition of power," Sata said amidst noise as his supporters kept disrupting his speech with slogans.

"It will be amiss of me if I don't acknowledge and thank my predecessor President Rupiah Banda's contribution to this transition," he said as the crowd cheered the outgoing President who was smiling at them.

The crowd constantly disturbed the flow of the speech.

"We must not allow violence to separate us. We are brothers and sisters," he declared.

"Our Noah" another placard read in reference to the new President cast as the Biblical Noah who moved the faithful to safety in the Ark during the floods after God had decided to destroy the world because of sin.

After the ceremony, the outgoing President drove back to State House while the presidential motorcade, with sirens blaring, escorted the new President to his Rhodespark home.

******

The outgoing President could no longer use the front entrance to State House that is reserved for the serving President and visiting dignitaries.

There is always a short military ceremony conducted at the main entrance when the President is either leaving or entering State House.

Schoolchildren marvel at the change of guard or when the President is passing through the gate. Neatly dressed soldiers perform a drill before standing still while the bugle is sounded.

At Nkhwazi House the former President was preparing to move out although his successor had told him to stay until government found a suitable home.

The country was back to normal and so was the traffic flow.

But the systematic attacks on MMD supporters increased. They were beaten and their homes looted that whole week following the conclusion of elections.

The police command had increased security at my home. It affected my children, as they didn't understand the sudden presence of guns around the home.

I continued going to the office to work on my handover notes.

"Everyone should stop reporting for work," the Chief of Staff said.

He was the only one to be present during that interim period because he feared the new team could harass us. But the secretary to the cabinet disagreed; we were expected to continue working normally until the President made changes.

On September 26, 2011, the outgoing President was to formally handover the office and staff to the incoming one.

We were all expected to line up just outside the President's office for the official handover. Even us the aides were supposed to be handed over to the new President.

The new President arrived at State House at about 10:00 hours.

The handover began with a tour of the buildings before senior aides were introduced to the new President.

"I want to start with the kitchen, where is the kitchen?" the new President asked as he greeted his predecessor at the entry to State House.

The two posed for a photo as they continued chatting.

"I have never been to the kitchen," the outgoing President said.

The two walked hand in hand from office to office.

"This is my friend," the new President told some State House waiters, referring to the outgoing President.

"I even buried his first wife when she died," he said.

The two walked on to the waiting aides.

The President greeted each one while making a comment or joke.

When he got to me, he shook my hand and moved on to the next person without making a comment.

The outgoing President was surprised because he knew we used to communicate when he was in the opposition.

"You mean you don't know Dickson Jere," he asked.

The new President stopped, walked a step backwards towards me.

"What?" he asked while pointing a finger at me.

"This boy from Matero," he answered, referring to the Lusaka township where I grew up alongside his sister and nephew.

I think he wanted to show that he knew me better from my childhood or he didn't want to show that he had spoken to me days earlier when he was declared the winner.

The next man in line was the Comptroller who introduced himself as an outgoing aide.

"No, you are not until I fire you," the new President said.

The outgoing President and his successor went into a closed-door meeting for the detailed handover. We were called in one by one for few consultations and left them to continue their discussion.

The last person to be called in was the president's personal physician, Dr. Shaileni Desai. He went into the meeting room and came out after a few minutes shaking his head with a smile on his face.

"I have been fired," he said while the rest of us burst into loud laughter.

"He told me I should go with the old-man so that I can continue looking after him," he said while joking that he had made history for being the first to be sacked from the old team.

I had prepared some talking notes for the outgoing President and on matters I wanted him to raise with his 'brother.' These included the continued attacks on MMD members and officials who were considered to have been close to the losing President.

"He has promised to stop the attacks," the outgoing President said after the two finished the talks.

"He also assured me that security will remain at your house until the situation calms down," he said.

When the official handover was over, I went to the office, bid farewell to my two assistants and my secretary.

"You were a fantastic team," I said. "Please, give the same support you gave me to the next person who will be appointed," I added.

My secretary inquired whether I had been formally dropped.

"No, not yet," I said.

I telephoned the secretary to the cabinet to inform him that I was taking days off but would be available should the new President require anything.

My other colleagues, Richard Chembe (Economics Advisor), and Joseph Jalasi (Legal) Francis Chigunta (Political) and Ben Kapita (Projects) decided to follow suit. Only the Chief of Protocol Bob Samakai reported for work after the handover.

The following day, we decided to have lunch with our former boss.

All his aides attended.

He was temporarily staying at a Lodge, called Number Eight Reedbuck in Kabulonga area.

"Congratulations Dr. Sichinga," the President said when he joined us at the table with his wife.

The new President had called him to ask for permission to appoint the Chief of Staff to another government position. Permission was granted and the chief of staff was now permanent secretary in the Ministry of Agriculture.

When the job was offered to Dr. Sichinga, he asked the new President to discuss the issue with his predecessor, as he was too close to the former.

"Even Bob has been appointed," the chief of staff said, informing us that our friend was taking up a new post as Permanent Secretary at the Ministry of Foreign Affairs.

The outgoing President looked surprised.

It was like his close aides had started abandoning him just one week after losing power.

"Who else?" he asked.

It turned out that only two accepted positions in the new administration.

After two weeks, the new President, as was expected, sacked three State House aides, namely Jalasi, Chigunta and Chembe.

My name was not on the list even though another person had taken up my job.

I telephoned cabinet office to check what was going on.

"I will check with the President. Your letter is not here," said Dr. Joshua Kanganja, secretary to cabinet who was in-charge of processing appointments and dismissals in the public service.

In the second week of October, I received the letter terminating my contract, which was personally signed by the new President.

But the nation was never told and many people thought I was still on the payroll awaiting redeployment.

CHAPTER TWENTY-ONE

THE MISSING GOLD

It was October 13, 2011– a few days after I officially left government.

I decided to catch up with old friends over a drink at my private office in Lusaka where I have a small bar. There were over a dozen guests from different backgrounds: lawyers, politicians, journalists, activists and businessmen. It was a reunion with my old friends whom I had been unable to see for a long time as a result of my State House job.

It was a party of single-malt whiskies, wines, shooters and beers while fumes from cigar puffs were all over. Then suddenly my phone rang.

"What have you done?" asked Joe Kaunda, who was now managing editor of *The Post* newspaper.

He was the only one missing from the party among the invited close friends.

"Please tune to the radio, the President is holding a press conference," he said before hanging up.

I alerted my guests and we tuned in to listen to the address. The President was accusing me and the former President's son, James, of having met a Swiss national, Nicholae Bogdan Buzaianu, who was under investigations over gold which the President said had gone missing.

The media put the value of the "missing gold" at US$ 7.5 million although experts said the value was exaggerated as it was not pure gold.

The accused, a Swiss businessman of Romanian origin, was a friend of Zambia. He was a known philanthropist who helped fund some community schools in Zambia. The President, during his tenure, appointed him Honorary Permanent Representative of Zambia to UNESCO due to his connections within that agency. He was a strong advocate for Zambia in UNESCO and organized the first-ever visit to Zambia of the UNESCO Director General, Irina Bokova.

The new President said the gold went missing during our time in government and that investigations into how it was disposed of had been launched. The Swiss businessman visited Zambia shortly after the change of government and met the former President before he took off in a private jet. It was widely reported that I was with the Swiss businessman when he got the gold before leaving the country.

"These people when they arrived were met by Dickson Jere and also by James Banda," the President said.

He said the Swiss businessman was wanted by the DEC and to have allowed him to fly out was wrong.

He then sacked the Lusaka police chief accusing him of failing to arrest the "fugitive" Swiss or ground his Jet.

"I need somebody who will be more alert," he said.

I could not believe my ears.

The President was totally misled by whoever gave him that information.

My guests began to excuse themselves, one by one and within a short time, almost all had left and I was alone in the office. I had instantly become a security risk and it wasn't difficult to realize that no one now wanted to be associated with me.

Even my buddy, James, who was at the party, left without telling me.

The President later sacked Buzaianu, saying he would replace him with a Zambian at UNESCO just days after he had demanded an apology and threatened to sue the Zambian government for defamation.

******

"*Sata Exposes Gold Scam*" was the headline in the morning newspapers as police swung into action to investigate and arrest those implicated in the deal.

"Retired President Rupiah Banda, his son and former press aide have been linked to a gold scam, said incumbent Michael Sata," was the headline in Kenya's *Daily Nation* newspaper.

A number of DEC employees were taken in for questioning as the gold was kept by the commission and we were supposed to have stolen it from there.

The truth was that the Zambian authorities had confiscated 119 kilograms of gold from some Zimbabwean nationals as they attempted to smuggle it through Zambia. They were arrested and jailed and the gold was forfeited to the state.

The culprits were in the news as they had attempted to bribe the judges to be released in return for a share of the proceeds from the sale.

"This case has generated a lot of interest from certain members of society who thought they could help the accused by offering all kinds of gifts and promising much more if the court ruled in their favour," said the Supreme Court judges when they found them guilty.

"This behaviour must be condemned in the strongest terms as it is an act in contempt of court in that it is calculated to interfere with the due process of the law. We shall not allow this to happen," the judges said.

The government decided to auction the gold through the DEC. It was bought by a Swiss company when we were still in office. However, allegations were made that I and the Swiss businessman had stolen the gold from DEC, which was bizarre. It came to light that in fact the sale was approved by the relevant government authorities and the contract of sale was approved by the Attorney General while the proceeds were paid into a government account.

I was deeply affected by the 'thief tag'.

******

The next few days were unpleasant.

My phone buzzed ceaselessly as the press sought my response.

My children were affected too as they were teased by friends at school over my alleged thieving. I may have my weakness but stealing has never been one of them.

It took a toll on my well-being as I kept to myself during that period. The only food I could stomach was green apples and I lost a lot of weight.

Concerned relatives camped at my home for solidarity.

The *Zambia Weekly* newsletter, in a very balanced story raised fundamental questions. "A real or invented gold scam" was the headline to its story. It reported that the inner circle of the former President was being turned upside down in an effort to trace an elusive batch of gold.

It confirmed that the gold was sold at the prevailing London Metal Exchange price and the money was paid into a government account and wondered whether Sata had been misled into calling it a scam.

The former President decided to respond.

"All the relevant people involved in this gold transaction are available and will provide all the necessary answers to the investigating team but suffice to say that no gold went missing mysteriously as has been portrayed," the statement released by his office said.

"President Banda is available at any given time to answer to any clarification which the current President may have concerning any issues before they are made public. This is the position he took when he made his farewell speech at State House after losing the last election," the statement said.

A week passed before I was summoned to appear before a joint investigations team made up of different security agencies.

"*Police summon Dickson Jere over Gold,*" read a headline in the *Zambian Watchdog* a day before my appearance.

It was a big story as a horde of journalists and photographers camped at the taskforce headquarters in Lusaka to cover my expected arrest and detention.

I arrived at exactly 14:00 hours in a window-tinted vehicle with my lawyer Sakwiba Sikota.

Police had a tough time clearing reporters and photographers who had blocked the gate while trying to get shots of me as I sat in the back seat.

I was upbeat.

I wore my trademark navy blue pinstripe suit, white shirt and polka dotted necktie with a pad of paper and pen in my hands. I was ready for the grilling or arrest.

A smartly dressed police officer in "civvies" welcomed us at the entrance to the huge double-storey building in Lusaka's Woodlands residential area, which was the centre for interrogations.

I had told my lawyer that I wanted to put a fight during the questioning.

"Let's wait and see what they have," he said while we waited at the reception.

The team was recording statements from the head of the treasury in the previous government, Likolo Ndalamei, over the same gold. Outgoing Attorney-General Abyudi Shonga was among those to be questioned.

"We are ready for you Mr. Jere," a youngish officer said as he ushered me into the conference room.

It was packed with several officers seated around the table.

I was offered a seat next to my lawyer as the head of the team introduced the group.

I scanned each face as names were disclosed.

"I want to explain before we begin the meeting," the head of the team said.

I was jotting down notes while my lawyer was on his laptop computer.

"We want to make it clear that there was no gold that was stolen or went missing." he began.

"We have called Mr. Jere here not as a suspect or possible witness... We just wanted to talk to him because his name has been mentioned several times but there is no evidence against him so far," he said.

The team wanted to hear from me and possibly record a statement.

"And nothing you are going to say will be used against you even in court," he assured me.

The explanation caught us off guard.

"In view of that, I request for a short adjournment to consult with my client," Sikota said.

We went outside and discussed with my lawyer and agreed that I should explain whatever I knew about the so-called "gold gate scandal".

When we went back, I took some questions before I signed a statement. I told the investigators what I knew about the gold. I informed them that I had received a call from someone in Switzerland who wanted to know whether it was true that Zambia was auctioning gold. I was not aware of that until he mentioned DEC as the institution that had put up the auction notice. I referred them to the DEC where they continued discussions. At that point, I was out of the picture and didn't even come to know how the negotiations went. I used to receive a lot of queries at State House and it was my role to refer people to the right offices.

Within 45 minutes, I was out.

The press gave chase as we drove off. They wanted an interview.

What is your comment Mr. Jere? How was the questioning?

"Interesting," I answered without elaboration.

The gold story ran for a while before it died down. Several officials were questioned over the same. The former DEC boss was subsequently arrested and charged for abuse of office in the manner that the sale was done while investigations into the matter were said to be continuing

"*Dickson Jere introduced gold buyers to ex-DEC commissioner,*" read a headline in *The Post* of November 7, 2011

The story said I introduced the buyers of the gold to the DEC after they met the President in Mfuwe. The story was based on unnamed 'intelligence sources' who quoted from part of my written statement to the probe team.

The newspaper also described me as "an errand boy" for the former President and that I had facilitated the gold deal for him. They demanded the former President be made personally accountable for the gold sale.

"Just spill the beans and be safe. You have a family to look after," some officials allied to the new government tried to cajole me to turn against my former boss.

I declined. As far as I knew, there was nothing to implicate him on.

The interesting twist to the story was that after the story did the rounds in the media my telephones and email were jammed with people who wanted me to buy their gold.

"I have 300 kilograms of pure gold. You can come and see it in Ghana," the emails said.

Others telephoned. I was mainly amused because I knew nothing about the gold trade and I could tell from the conversations that some of them were conmen.

But there it was; I had become a gold dealer by implication.

CHAPTER TWENTY-TWO
THERE IS LIFE AFTER PRESIDENCY

The former President sat in a wood paneled dock in the Lusaka magistrate's court.

He was calm and occasionally smiled at his relatives, friends and supporters who packed the tiny courtroom on March 26, 2013.

He was an accused person and was appearing in court on the first day of trial.

"Not guilty," he said when asked how he was pleading to the charge of corruption and abuse of office.

Outside the courtroom, police battled with scores of his supporters who demonstrated against the arrest of the former President.

He had since leaving office kept himself busy with international engagements ranging from observing elections to lecturing on African democracy. His international profile had risen rapidly and he was the recipient of a number of awards for promoting good governance and democracy in Africa.

But the new government made no secret of the fact that they considered him a "thief." They opened an array of investigations into his three-year stewardship which they claimed was characterized by corruption and theft of public funds.

He was summoned to appear before the Anti-Corruption Commission but he refused on the grounds that as a former head of state he enjoyed constitutional immunity against prosecution.

His wife, Thandiwe, was also the subject of investigations. It was said that the trust she established for the couple's twins had built blocks of flats in Lusaka in unclear circumstances. It was claimed that financing for the project was acquired from dubious sources. She was questioned by police and subsequently government restricted the property. However, the Lusaka High Court varied the order after she appealed.

"Information we have received is that the Mpundu Trust is holding over US$1 million with local banks. I strongly believe that it's only fair and prudent for law enforcement agencies to professionally and systematically investigate this matter," said Sata in a statement.

The said money was a loan from Access Bank of Nigeria.

The anticorruption NGO Transparency International Zambia (TIZ) joined in calling for the arrest of the former President. It called for national street demonstrations around the country to press for his arrest.

"It is not a bad precedent to lift a former head of state's immunity to face prosecution if indeed he was involved in stealing from the same people he was expected to serve," said Goodwell Lungu in a statement.

"It is always TIZ's conviction that men and women who elect to become heads of state in Zambia should always be above board and not assume such offices with criminal intentions," he said.

The government also accused him of having used state funds to finance the 2011 campaign.

On March 15, 2013, government quite unexpectedly moved a motion in the National Assembly to strip him of his constitutional immunity against prosecution so that he could be arrested and stand trial.

There was chaos in the House as opposition lawmakers attempted to disrupt the proceedings before finally staging a walkout in protest at the motion.

"It has now been established that cash was personally disbursed by Rupiah Banda and his family and that the MMD never had such sums of money in its bank account at any time," the Justice Minister Wynter Kabimba told parliament.

"Mr. Banda's personal handling of such large sums of money and his activities constitute money laundering.... for which he is liable to prosecution," he said.

The national assembly, in the absence of the opposition voted to remove the immunity.

The former President was subsequently questioned for several hours before being arrested for abuse of office over an oil procurement contract with a Nigerian company. The charge stated that he abused his authority by procuring oil on behalf of the country when the proceeds were intended for his benefit and members of his family.

The former President was later charged with another offence of "concealing gratification" for receiving campaign vehicles from a Chinese company that had contracts with the government.

Despite worsening climate for the former President at home international invitations continued. But each time he left the country, there were attempts to twist his purposes. When he traveled to South Africa for meetings, President Sata said his predecessor was seeking political asylum. He warned that government would still extradite him and bring him to face criminal charges.

The former President responded.

"I wholly reject this deliberate misinformation. I have been on a trip that was planned long ago and I intend to return to Zambia. Any statements that have been made regarding fabricated ideas of asylum have no basis in fact," he said.

At around the same time the Zambian opposition held a media briefing in South Africa where they petitioned the Commonwealth to investigate the escalating cases of human rights abuses in Zambia following the change of government. They tabulated all the alleged abuses in a document that they circulated.

The Sata government blamed that briefing on the former President and the official government spokesman said I had traveled to South Africa with the former President to organize political meetings with Zambian opposition leaders with the aim of embarrassing the government. But I was not on that trip and never attended any meetings.

From then on the government's attitude to the former President's foreign travel seemed to harden.

He was invited for the inauguration of Kenyan President Uhuru Kenyatta, but government blocked the trip. They denied him access to his passport which was held by the court as part of his bail conditions. He was granted permission to travel by the court after an application.

However, despite the court action immigration officers refused to process his departure on April 9, 2013. He was accompanied by his wife and aides. He obliged and returned home.

"Rule of law clearly no longer exists," said Robert Amsterdam, his international lawyer.

"When a government brazenly ignores its courts and uses violence against its own citizens, society is exposed to the worst kinds of abuses of power that can lead to atrocities," he added.

The Law Association of Zambia (LAZ) and other civic organizations condemned the government's disregard of a lawful court order.

"...The steps taken by the Immigration Officers to block Mr. Banda from traveling abroad are not only illegal but they directly border on contempt of Court," said George Chisanga, LAZ vice President.

"We wish to earnestly urge the relevant government authorities to immediately ensure that Mr. Banda's passage is facilitated so that the ruling of the High Court is given legal efficacy," he said.

After the abortive Kenya trip, there was an invitation from Boston University to attend an African Roundtable discussion in June 2013 in South Africa. He was expected to chair a session alongside other former African presidents.

Once more, he applied to the court for permission to travel and once again it was granted. At the airport accompanied by his wife, Immigration officers would not again process his departure. When shown the court order they said they were also acting on "orders from above." They would not budge and the trip had to be aborted.

He was livid.

"When I was President I did not do this to anybody. If I had done something like that my conscience would not be clear," the former President said.

"I am not heartbroken by these persecutions. I have to be strong," he told reporters at the airport.

Prior to the South African trip, he was also denied permission to travel to Tanzania where President Jakaya Kikwete had invited him to attend the 2013 Global Smart Partnership Forum.

Government said they considered him a "flight risk" even after the court had granted him permission to leave the country. His diplomatic passport was later confiscated and canceled.

"The investigations team has imposed travel embargoes against the former President for fear that he might interfere with witnesses," Home Affairs Minister Edgar Lungu revealed.

******

The new government carried out a sustained negative campaign against the former President since he left office. He was depicted as a corrupt man who was involved in several questionable deals with members of his family. The government also threatened to withhold his benefits unless he quit his position as MMD president because the law prohibited former presidents from engaging in active politics.

The new President threw in more dirt.

He accused the former President of having stolen two luxury Lexus vehicles from the State House pool. It was alleged that they were ordered but never arrived. The former President explained that he was not aware of such transactions, as he was not a procurement officer.

But President Sata stuck to his guns:

"Those vehicles I told you about two days ago were not only two but four. They have only delivered two. The State paid for four vehicles," he said.

"And there was no tender for those vehicles." That opened the way for anti-corruption activists to call for the arrest of the former President for corruption and abuse of office.

"Lift Rupiah Banda's Immunity," demanded Transparency International Zambia, as pressure began to mount on lawmakers to remove the former President's constitutional immunity against prosecution.

Some of the ministers who worked with the former President jumped ship and joined the new government.

Several commissions of inquiry were appointed by the new President immediately he assumed office. They were tasked to probe various transactions of the former administration and the former President was being implicated endlessly. But no tangible evidence was forthcoming, only accusations. But the media relished the stories.

The President again accused his predecessor of having awarded a contract to a Turkish company, Guris Holdings, to build a new international airport in Lusaka without following tender procedure.

"I am therefore suspending or canceling these contracts. I don't see any urgency of having a new airport." he said.

"We will go to tender if there is need for a new airport," he said.

The President also unilaterally canceled a project to construct a new State House, which his predecessor had begun.

"Surprisingly, this place is more than adequate," the President said, referring to the State House.

The new President reversed the sale of Zamtel, the state-owned telecommunication company where the majority stake had been sold to the Libyan company – LAP Green Network. It was alleged that there was corruption in the sale and he accused the former President and his family of having benefitted.

But the former President had magnanimously handed over power and internationally continued to be seen as an example of an African leader ready to play by the rules of democracy. Former US President Jimmy Carter was the first to recognize his pedigree and made him leader of the Carter Center Election Observation Mission to the Democratic Republic of Congo (DRC).

I accompanied him on that mission.

"There is life after Presidency," he said as the audience gave him a standing ovation with a huge round of applause.

"Here I am, doing another task for Africa," he told officials from the Congolese National Election Commission (CENI) and local election observers when he paid a courtesy call at their offices.

He had been out of office only two months when he was in the Congo to monitor the November 28, 2011 elections.

It was that assignment that gave us the early hint that even though "there is life after Presidency", it was going to be rough.

The new President refused to allow him travel with his bodyguards, although he is entitled to 24 hours protection under the terms of retirement for former Presidents.

"I will travel without them," he told me while joking that I should be ready to act as his aide as well as his bodyguard while in the Congo.

Some of his friends decided to foot the expenses of his bodyguards after government allowed them to travel if the former President would pay. In Congo, the government of President Joseph Kabila Kabange provided additional security as he toured the volatile areas in Kinshasa ahead of the elections.

He fitted the role and played peacemaker as well.

CENI used him to meet candidates to calm the situation down as tempers rose over persistent reports of vote-rigging and manipulation. Most candidates spoke to him quickly and saw a model in him.

"You are a rare breed in Africa," said Etienne Tshisekedi wa Mulumba, a veteran politician and former Prime Minister who was the presidential candidate for the Union for Democracy and Social Progress.

The former President met him over his party's threats to disrupt the elections on the grounds that President Kabila had rigged the vote. The mission to Congo was a success and after peaceful elections, won by President Kabila, we traveled back home.

At that time, the former President was toying with the idea of forming a foundation to promote Democracy and Good Governance in Africa.

But before the plans could be elaborated another invitation came in to be the African President-in-Residence lecturer at Boston University in the US on a program designed for African Presidents who left power in a democratic way.

On its website, the university credited him with overseeing significant national growth rates during his tenure with the GDP peaking at 7.6 percent in 2010 and said of him that he had only narrowly lost re-election in September 2011.

"Center Director Charles Stith says there is much to learn from Banda's experience in pulling Zambia out of the global recession," it further reported.

He was the eighth African leader to participate in that programme. Others were former President of Zanzibar Abeid Amani Karume, former President of Cape Verde Antonio Monteiro, the former Presidents of Botswana Festus Mogae and Sir Ketumire Masire, former Liberian President Ruth Perry and former Zambian President Kenneth Kaunda.

The Boston program required him to be away for about three months, which meant his party, the MMD, would remain leaderless for that period. He decided to quit the party position and called a news conference to announce his resignation.

When his Boston stint was over, another international assignment was waiting. He was to lead an election observer mission to the Kingdom of Lesotho elections under the auspices of the Electoral Institute for Sustainable Democracy in Africa (EISA).

I was with him on that mission.

The Zambian government refused to finance his trip saying there was no money although there is a budget line for the offices of former Presidents.

It was an interesting outing where he mingled with former President like Bakili Muluzi of Malawi and General Yakubu Gowon of Nigeria.

He was again the leader of the Carter Centre Election Observation Mission to the Kenya elections which saw the election of President Kenyatta. He is the recipient of a number of international awards among them: the Crans Montana Prix de la Foundation Award based in Switzerland and later the Honorary Prize for African Democracy at the 2012 Lifetime Africa Achievement Awards in Kenya.

Back home, the government described the awards as "fake" saying he did not deserve them.

"Rupiah Banda is a thief and wanted to steal elections," said Wynter Kabimba, Zambia's Justice Minister.

The former President was later admitted to the prestigious Club de Madrid, a club of former Presidents created to promote democracy and change in the world.

So, he was in a sense right: there is life after the presidency however fraught it is.

CHAPTER TWENTY-THREE
MY REFLECTIONS

What went wrong?

Why did President Rupiah Banda lose the 2011 election when outwardly so much was in his favour? This is the question that has spooked many analysts and observers of the Zambian political scene.

Right up to the last minute many gave him the edge. He had so smoothly and effectively presided over one of the fastest growing economies in sub-Saharan Africa and all indicators on the ground remained positive.

It has to be said though that the defeat was a rather narrow one- Sata the winner was on 42.24% and Banda on 35.63%. But it was a defeat nevertheless and was quite unexpected given for instance the macro-economic fundamentals:

Single-digit inflation, economic growth that averaged around seven percent per year and a stable exchange rate. Food prices were manageable and the agricultural harvests during his tenure were among the highest recorded in the country's history. There was also a general sense of forward momentum after many years of stagnation- new schools, hospitals and roads were being opened. But still the voters would not endorse the incumbent.

In this Chapter, I share some of my views based on the inside reading of what could have gone wrong.

From the outset, we all knew that the 2011 election was going to be a tight race between the top two candidates. Opinion polls conducted by the British Consultants – Bell Pottinger – consistently showed that the race was going to be tight and recommended certain decisions to be made if the President was to win the election. I was the only one at State House who was privy to the findings, which were always presented to a carefully assembled group of some trusted lieutenants, family members as well as two ministers.

The first hurdle, which clearly came out at that stage was that, the MMD could have overstayed its welcome in power. It had been in office for two decades and Zambians naturally longed for change.

We tried to brand the President as a new man representing *"stability, security and prosperity"* for all. However, the message of change had gained momentum and was popular and the opposition capitalized on it well.

Zambians believed that the MMD had had their time just like UNIP, the party that led the independence struggle, which ruled for 27 years and was booted out in 1991. The opposition also used "outright lies" to excite young voters to their side.

Sata promised to create jobs for all the unemployed youths within 90 days of coming to office. It was good-sounding populist rhetoric that excited many. But the MMD seemed to take those promises as a joke. How could one conceivably achieve such a feat in so short a time? The party expected voters to see through it all. In the end though they did not seem to!

But the major role in the defeat was probably played by changes to the composition of the voter roll. For the first time since the 2006 election, the voters' roll had a number of first-time voters, mainly young people either in colleges or unemployed. The British Consultants raised this factor as a threat as first time voters were historically known to vote for the opposition.

Although the MMD tried to address the young voters, the message does not seem to have been strong enough to win them over.

Further, the President who had come out of political retirement was unknown to most young people compared to Sata who had been in opposition consistently for 10 years. Most of the new voters were in traditional opposition strongholds of Lusaka, Copperbelt and Northern provinces while the MMD areas lagged behind.

The new voters roll had 1,064,730 first-time voters, mainly youths, out of the total number of the 5,167,154 registered voters. The 2006 register, which was used in the 2008 presidential elections, which the President won had 3,940,053 million voters.

******

The President's stronghold in western province was also shaken as a result of the handling of the secession movement in the province. It was an old issue but one that appeared to gain momentum during the President's time. The situation was tense in the province and the opposition took advantage of the fallout between government and some of the activists from the area. Opposition leader Michael Sata travelled to the province and assured the people that he would grant them their wish if they elected him President. Support for the MMD weakened in the area which had traditionally voted MMD. There had been a riot over secession in the provincial capital Mongu and police used live ammunition to quell the looting, which led to the death of two protesters. The President was squarely blamed for the deaths.

"*Rupiah is a murderer!*" read a placard displayed by youths who attempted to blockade the presidential motorcade when he visited the area shortly before the elections. Objects were thrown at the motorcade forcing police to use teargas to disperse the unruly youths.

When voting came, the province was split and all the three major parties took a bite of the ballots, which narrowed the President's slice.

*****

Another issue that came out strongly in the opinion poll was that of violence in the capital, Lusaka and some parts of the Copperbelt Province. There was a perception that the violence was the work of the President's supporters even when evidence showed otherwise. It was the work of the opposition. Even though the President talked tough to the party leadership on the need to end the violence, he did not take strong measures such as dismissing some of the leaders linked to violence. The perception contributed to increased support for the opposition, especially in the capital, Lusaka.

The poll also indicated that the President was seen to be soft when it came to dealing with corruption. The Consultants had insisted that the President should take strong measures including sacking some of the officials linked to the vice, with or without evidence purely on a political basis. The President, as was his character, refused to do that. He insisted on evidence before he could mete out any punishment. The head to head poll between the President and his archrival Sata showed the President trailing by far with respect to corruption. Zambians believed at the time that Sata was better placed to deal with corruption, which the President appeared to tolerate.

The issue of corruption was mainly perception created by the private media. The President was aware of that and it was the reason for his insistence on doing things right based on evidence. In the end, the perception grew and voters believed the President was tolerant of corruption.

****

The choice of the campaign manager and the entire campaign team was another factor the impacted the election outcome. The President picked a junior Minister, Dr. Boniface Kawimbe as his campaign manager replacing veteran politician and Chief Whip Vernon Mwaanga (VJ) who was sacked just before the campaign started. The removal of VJ did not go well within the party rank and file. It impacted negatively on morale in the party.

The removal of VJ was premised on the fact that he had a bad reputation when it came to managing elections. He was believed to be an election rigger and the President wanted someone with a clean name in his team. Others questioned the rationale in choosing a deputy minister to be in-charge of the national campaign when he had several senior Cabinet Ministers who could have taken up that role. Despite being a junior minister, Kabimbe had no track record in running an election and was away from local politics for a while after he went on a sabbatical in the US.

I once approached the President on the choice of his campaign manager.

"I hear you but we have already decided. We can't keep changing managers..." the President responded.

He had seen the point I raised on appointing a junior minister to take charge of such a mammoth task. Others who were appointed in the campaign team had no previous experience of running a campaign. The President's son, Henry, took a leading role, something that upset some party stalwarts. Issues were raised on why the President's son who had no position in the party was playing a key role in the campaign while there existed well-staffed machinery. In the end, the impression created was that the party machinery was sidelined.

"We have been in this party from inception, we have never seen the President's children take charge of election campaigns. They need to help from a distance," a senior party official observed.

I recall party national secretary, Richard Kachingwe, raising a complaint with me that the President had ignored the entire party machinery in establishing the Campaign Centre. This meant that most resources were channeled to the centre rather than to party structures. The campaign team also devised strict rules of acquiring resources for the campaign. Candidates were made to personally sign for the materials they collected. This caused problems for candidates from far-flung areas – they had to abandon the campaign and travel to Lusaka for the materials.

****

The party leadership at provincial level was heavily divided. The President made the greatest mistake when he imposed the leadership of the party in all the provinces, except Southern Province where he allowed a free contest. Members wanted incumbent provincial party committees out of office prior to the elections. The dominant perception was that they had overstayed in their positions. They were also accused of stifling party growth. I personally was for the idea that the party should choose its leadership in a free and fair contest. The President thought otherwise.

There were cases where popular candidates were made to withdraw from the race in order to allow unpopular ones to go through unopposed. In some instances, the party members disagreed with the President's choice and walked out of the electoral conferences, which eventually affected party performance. By the time the President was going for elections, most members had lost faith in the party leadership at the provincial level. "I will not join the campaign, I will watch from the terraces," one popular party member once told me after he was made to withdraw from the nomination contest. The provincial party teams were expected to be the extension of the President's campaign. However, most of them did not support him because they saw him as imposing unpopular leaders on the party.

The President took a similar stance at the party National Convention, which was held a few months before the General Elections. He had a list of those he wanted elected to top positions and rejected others. In some cases, he had genuine reasons for his choices. He wanted the party top leadership to be balanced regionally and therefore asked some senior members from the Eastern province, his home area to withdraw their nomination since he was already elected unopposed as party president. Despite massive persuasion, some members openly rejected his political manoeuvring and ended up electing some of those he opposed. Some ministers and party leaders for instance supported a former Minister Sylvia Masebo for the position of Women chairperson when she was not on the President's list. She won convincingly and the President had difficulties working with her. She would later resign to join the opposition Patriotic Front just before elections.

I tried to bridge the wedge between the President and Masebo. I visited her twice to try and help make peace between the two. She is a personal friend and she was frank with me and said that she felt the President didn't want her near the campaign. Suspicion between them only grew by the day. Her resignation was a big blow to the Presidential team as media reports indicated serious fallout in the party ahead of the general elections.

****

In retrospect, we advisors were also culprits as well. We did not handle the President's diary well. Throughout his tenure party activities were never a priority. There had for instance been a proposal from the party that Wednesdays should be devoted to party matters in consultation with the secretariat but that never happened. Mistrust developed between State House and the party leadership, which sometimes led to bitter exchanges in public. We in State House overloaded the President with so many national issues and rarely allowed him to interact with the party except when the National Executive Committee (NEC) meetings were scheduled ahead of a by-election or to expel some truant member. Whilst Cabinet met every week, NEC only met when there was an issue. At times months could pass without any meeting.

"You should remember that without a party, you won't be in State House," was the line we often got from the party leadership.

Even within State House, coordination was disorganized among the aides. We had no weekly meetings to plan for the President's diary and programmes. From my recollection, in three years, we only had three staff meetings. Planning was left to me, Chief of Staff, Principal Private Secretary and the Chief of Protocol. The rest of the aides were usually in the dark about what was going on. I wasn't even "supposed" to be in these meetings. I merely imposed myself on the team because I realized that I needed to know every move of the President if I had to speak of his behalf effectively. Further, some of the foreign trips we committed the President to took him away from involvement in domestic politics was required. The value of some of these trips was questionable. With hindsight, we should have slowed down the pace of foreign travel especially in the face of accusations that the President was spending more time in the air than at home.

Inside the Presidency

Another issue that the aides failed to sort out was the sudden change of work schedules caused by his knee operation he had in Cape Town. In his first year, the President was, for all practical purposes, a real workaholic. He reported for work at 08:00 hours and left office close to midnight. This meant that all of us, with the exception of the Chief of Staff, stayed in the office until we bid goodnight to the principal.

Following the operation in 2010, his medical team recommended a few months of rest Consequently, the President's work schedule changed drastically. He steadily cut his office hours and preferred to work from home. This meant that his staff had to follow him to his official residence and meetings used to take place there. The house was not conducive for official meetings as it was designed as a residence. This matter became one of the talking points within the Presidency and security people but there was no one who really took it up seriously with the President. Visiting family members could accidentally enter a meeting if not warned. As per African culture, they would end up shaking hands with everyone thereby disturbing the meeting.

"DJ please raise this matter with the President. I think you are the only one who can take on the President on such thorny issues," one of the Principal Private Secretaries once requested. But it was one of the issues I never wanted to raise with my boss. I thought the Chief of Staff was better suited to bring it up.

The President's working from home gave ammunition to his enemies when they came to know about it. They branded him as lazy and portrayed him as spending most of his time at home roasting meat. In fact one of his former ministers, Mike Mulongoti even went to the press to accuse the President of spending too much of his time at home unlike his predecessors. I had to call a news conference to rebut the accusations.

"The President has a fully fledged office at his residence. Those who have been there can attest to this," I told the press. But my statement only attracted further counsel from former Vice President Enock Kavindele who advised that it was a bad precedent for the President to be meeting "strangers" at his residence.

To further heighten this negative perception, the President started missing cabinet meetings as he concentrated on other pressing issues with technocrats. This is despite delegating chairing of meetings to his Vice President. At times, he would open the meeting and leave after a few hours for other engagements. This prompted speculations that he had lost interest in running government. When the President handled the cabinet meetings, they would run for several hours and a lot of issues came up during debates, prompting action. This is unlike when the Vice President took charge. Meetings could end within 30 minutes. Ministers lost interest. Some of the ministers who were allied to the President raised this issue with me saying he was losing grip by asking his deputy to handle such meetings. As I mentioned in earlier Chapters, the President preferred to work with small cabinet committees, which were effective, and result oriented. He picked ministers according to their portfolio and education background depending on an issue to be addressed.

****

"This was not a takeover…" was the answer the President always gave when asked why he had not made changes in key positions, including in the defence and security forces after he won the elections in 2008. "It is the same party in power," he added, saying he had not taken over government from another political party for him to do major surgery to the government. With few changes, the President maintained the same cabinet, which his predecessor, the late Levy Mwanawasa had. He also left the military commanders in their positions. Some ministers used that to show total disloyalty to the President saying he did not appoint them. Many had advised the President, including Cabinet Office that he should dissolve the entire cabinet and constitute his own team. "This is not a takeover…" the President responded with usual refrain to such advice. So very few ministers took oath and pledged allegiance to him.

Within the defence forces, the junior ranks were not happy that the President maintained the commanders who had reached retirement age but were given contracts to continue thereby stifling promotions at the lower ranks. Anonymous letters started arriving at my desk as well as newspapers indicating low morale in the defence forces due to stagnation in promotions.

"We shall not vote for President Rupiah Banda if he does not fire the Commanders who are on contract to pave way for young officers to raise…" one of the letters read in part. Some graffiti were even spotted in some army cantonment. One year into office, the President's popularity had dwindled within the defence forces. This is despite implementing key infrastructure projects such as building new houses for the soldiers.

"Tell the President, all these projects won't make any difference to the men in uniform. They need promotions," one officer openly advised me.

The President only acted a year after he came to office at a press conference on April 7, 2010. He took the bold decision to sack all the top military commanders. However, he opened a new line of attack in the air force when he appointed a new commander, who had been retired, which was seen to defeat the whole purpose of the exercise. Further, he retained the Inspector General of police Francis Kabonde and Director General of the intelligence Regis Phiri. The fired Generals were redeployed into diplomatic service.

****

These are some of the few issues that I perceived to have contributed to the defeat of the President notwithstanding his good economic management, which he presided over. I believe outcomes would have been different if these issues had been addressed promptly. However, as they say, hindsight is 20-20. In the middle of the heat of political activity, such clarity would be muddled.

Some of my colleagues may have different opinions on these issues. I hope they will write their version too!

Ends!

www.ingramcontent.com/pod-product-compliance
Lightning Source LLC
Chambersburg PA
CBHW022006220426
43663CB00007B/982